THE EVENTFUL LIFE

OF

NATHANIEL DALE,

WITH

Recollections & Anecdotes

CONTAINING

A great variety of Business Matters,
&c., as occurred in the life of the
Author.

———◆———

SEVEN YEARS PARK-KEEPER AND BAILIFF TO THE RIGHT
HON. LADY WILLOUGHBY DE ERSBY, GRIMSTHORPE,
LINCOLNSHIRE;

FIFTEEN YEARS WITH WILLIAM FIFTH DUKE OF
MANCHESTER, AND SEVEN WITH GEORGE SIXTH
DUKE OF MANCHESTER, KIMBOLTON ;

TEN YEARS TENANT FARMER UNDER THE EARL OF
HARBOROUGH AT SAXBY;

TWO YEARS AS SALESMAN IN THE LIVE STOCK
MARKET, LONDON;

AND THE LAST SEVEN YEARS AS A RESIDENT IN
KIMBOLTON.

———◆———

PRINTED (LITERALLY) FOR THE AUTHOR, OF WHOM ONLY COPIES
CAN BE HAD. CLOTH, 2/6. PAPER, 1/6.

CONTENTS.

———o———

CONTENTS.

CHAPTER IV.

At Kimbolton—A Change of Beast, Sheep, Bucks, and Does—Venison and Game given away by the Duke—Stabbed by a Buck—Training my Horse and Dog—Change of Spaniels—Selling and buying horses without a warrant—Rabbits given to me by the Duke Our plan found out by a Lawyer, and the information taken to the Duke by the Parson—Killing rabbits at Shelton—The offals of the deer taken from the Steward, and given to me by the Duke—A Buck killed in Honey Hill Wood—The Duke meets with the Parson—Taking a wife—The Duke nearly being shot by Squire Fletcher—The Duke out at half-past Two o'clock in the morning—Old Grant knocking down his wife and daughter—The Duke's kindness to old Grant—My best Gun made by Mr. Bull of Bedford—My first Gambling—My Opinion of the New Education Act.

CHAPTER V.

The Right Hon. Lord Willoughby and Polly Clapton's pigstye—My way of choosing and buying a horse—Training my horse to follow me—The Duke's remark about children and dogs—In trouble with a girl at Nottingham—Killing a Buck on Sunday—Mr. George with his men at the Election at Huntingdon—Thrashing the Blue Party.

CHAPTER VI.

Draining the home farm and park—Making the large fish pond—Nearly drowned therein afterwards—The groom riding after the bucks—The present Duke of Manchester—First turn at fawn shooting—Attacked by a buck—Wood pigeon shooting—Race with the footman—Farmers in trouble about the rooks—The rope round the Duke's neck—All but a fight with the butler—A day's shooting with Mr. L. J. Ibbs—The groom contending with the Duke—The Duke's joke about the spaniels—Hornsby fighting the spud—The way Jimmy Dean cleaned his teeth—Grass for a jack rabbit—The Duke and the woman in family-way—Gipsies eating hedge hogs—An attempt to stop me on my return from Bedford—Wild duck shooting—The late Duke taking possession—The change of Stewards—The death of the late Duchess—Killing rats and mice—My first day's hunt with the present Duke of Manchester and Lord Robert Montague—Leaving Kimbolton.

CHAPTER VII.

Taking the Inn and Land at Castle Bytham—Rough work with the navvies—The race—A dispute about the agreement—Taking a farm under the Earl of Harborough—Rotten sheep—Favors from the Earl —Taking rabbits from the drains—The lung complaint among the beast—Summoned for offering bad meat—Curing a bullock of the lung complaint—All my crops lost by fire—Great kindness from the Rev. Mapelton and his lady—The death of my daughter—The death of the Earl of Harborough—Favors from the Countess—No favors from the Steward and Markham—The Agreement signed—My leaving Saxby.

CHAPTER VIII.

Two years as Cattle Salesman in the London Market—The reason of stock being turned out unsold—One reason why meat is so dear— My second marriage—The Irish employed—The wagoner and the prize-fighter—The deceitful Neighbour---saving the grey mare.

CHAPTER IX.

My return to Kimbolton—Meeting with the present Duke of Manchester—Killing the leveret—The Rev. T. Ainsworth in trouble— Our return from Stow—My favourite song—A joke with Rev. P. P. —Marriage of my daughters, Gertrude and Eliza—A day with the hounds—The Prince and Princess of Wales at the Castle—Mr. Lintott's fall—Our visit to Grimsthorpe—Beautiful cows—A visit to Careby—The ducks—Fine beast—The village I was chased through —Well entertained at the Willoughby Arms—To Peterborough— Mistake with the Fly—Feeding the fish—My dog Pilot—Grantley Berkeley losing his bet—Our visit to Stow—The wool buyer at Leicester—The Rev. Hog and his billy—Mr. Horsford in scarlet-- Painting the toll collector—The Marquis' horse jumping the hurdle in the dining room—A keeper's dodge with the partridge's eggs— The country farmer's first visit to London—Giving the sow a drink —The old lady's mistake in travelling by rail—Old Croger and his quid of tobacco—A strange stag in the park—Catching a buck asleep —My dog on watch—A hunt in the dark—The lady and her nursemaid—Meeting the daughters of an old friend—Tally-o in chapel— The clerk and the Duke's strong ale—Footman choked with a beefsteak—Lord Frederick locked out.

Now Ready.

N. Dale has also caused to be printed over Seventy Recipes, which have been collected at a great expense, and proved by him upwards of forty years.

He has circulated a few among his friends, who have borne unqualified testimony to their excellence, stating they would not be without the oils in their houses under any consideration.

Some excellent and most valuable Recipes for the Household are also included.

To be had of the Compiler,

HIGH STREET, KIMBOLTON.

PREFACE.

When I first began to write the following pages, I intended it to be printed and given to my children only; but as it became known to my friends and neighbours, and many having expressed a wish to be supplied with copies, I have been persuaded upon to bring out a larger number, so that it may be offered to the public generally.

Should the contents, all of which are facts that have occured during my life, be accepted by the public, I hope it may be the means of exciting the mind of some of my readers, not only to industry in business, but to prepare for the world to come.

I hope and trust that all my readers will sympathise with the interest I have felt in my little work, and pardon all mistakes that occur therein.

THE AUTHOR.

ERRATA.

Page 14, line 30, *for* Caveby *read* Careby.
  ,, 15, lines 13 and 17, *for* Caveby *read* Careby.
  ,, 48, line 7, *for* me *read* him.
  ,, 48, ,, 9, *for* him *read* me.
  ,, 49, ,, 12, *for* I *read* We.
  ,, 72, ,, 4, *for* two *read* twelve.

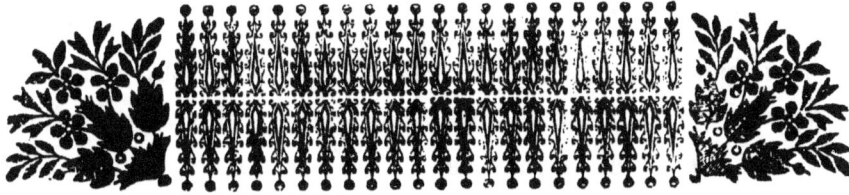

THE
LIFE AND RECOLLECTIONS
OF
NATHANIEL DALE.

CHAPTER I.
BIRTH, PARENTAGE, AND EARLY DAYS.

WAS born at Little Bytham, Lincolnshire, on the 12th of October, 1805. My father was a steady and industrious man, occupying a small portion of land with other business. I was the third of eleven children, and as soon as possible was trained for business of different kinds. My mother was fond of flowers, and imbibed good choice and management from her relatives, Her father being bailiff for Squire Reynordson of Holywell Hall; and

Her eldest brother, a gardener & seedsman in the High Street, Stamford. My uncle Nathaniel and name-sake was clerk to Mr. Wiche, solicitor, Barnhill, Stamford. At the time the savings' bank was opened he was chosen to be the Manager of it, where he remained until his death. The time he held the office was over twenty years. He was also clerk to the Magistrates. But to return: I was often set to work in the garden as soon as they could make me know a flower-plant or shrub from a weed. As I frequently made mistakes, I was sent to school to Mrs. Frisby, but better known as Nanny Frisby: she was a widow, with one married daughter at home to assist, as she had a cottage, kept two cows, pigs, geese, and a donkey, with a grocer's shop, and baked bread and dinners for the parish. They found plenty to do, and to occupy their leisure time, there were always two wheels in the house to sit down to, for they always spun their own flax and hemp, to weave into linen for their family use. Their charge per head for their pupils was three-pence per week. During the winter months I used to take a bit of wood with me on a Monday, as she made no charge for firing or extras of any kind. After I had been there three or four weeks, I was reported to be the most unruly boy in the school, which numbered from eight to twelve, the girls complaining that I would not let them get on with their work. Orders then came from Misses that each boy should learn to knit or stitch, I chose the latter. As I was about six years old, I was to take needle, thread, thimble, and cloth of some kind to practice upon between times for our lessons. So thing spassed on for about two years, at the end of which time I held a good character, and was competent to back-stitch, hem, fell, sew on a button, and work a button hole. which Mrs. Frisby said I should find very useful after leaving my mother, and I must confess I did.

I must tell the readers of this work we were allowed two half holidays during each week, but I was not allowed to play about in the street, as others of my school fellows. There was always a job for me, either to nurse the baby, rock the cradle, or to rub some of the old fashioned furniture, until I could see my face in it, after the girls had smeared it over with bees-wax and turpentine; or should we have had a load of wood or coal brought home, and tumbled out of the carts, to be carried at the men's leisure. When they had moved the chief part, my eldest brother, (who was about two years older than myself) and I were told to pick every bit up as large as a bird's eye or bees knee. I must confess it was almost too much for my mettle.

About this time I got into sad disgrace. Another baby born, my grandmother came to attend to my mother and look after the duties of the house. One tea-time I noticed her cutting the bread and butter, when a little dash of snuff fell from her nose upon a portion of it, as at that time some of the old ladies took a great deal of it, and she consumed her share. When we came to the tea table, I refused my bread and butter; my father wished to know the cause. I told him I should not eat of the bread and butter cut by my grandmother, without she left off taking snuff, consequently I had to go without as I dare not tell what I had seen in her presence.

Some time after I was sent to the baker's at the other end of the Village for a white loaf, which I received from the baker; before I got half-way home, being hungry I had picked all the corners off the loaf and a great deal of the inside, so much, that I dare not take it home, so I threw the remainder into a bunch of nettles ; as a matter of course I was severely punished as it was soon found out; although it is sixty years since, I could go to the exact spot.

Some days after a lady asked me how my mother and baby were getting on. I told her very well. She said, how do you like the baby. I said, very well. But I wished the baby had not come, as I had heard my mother say she could not make the sugar and butter hold out from week to week, and I thought I should not get any now ; the lady often told me of it after.

About that time, Bill Swingler, my only companion, and I, were passing the orchard of a woman named Mary Daff, commonly called Molly Daff: she called us in to get her some plums, which we gladly agreed to do. After we had gathered her what she required, she said you can go now, as I must shut the gate. I said, I hope you will give us a few plums Molly, for our trouble. Well, she said, I can only give you one between you, so she divided one between us ; after that we called her old Split-plum, a name she was known by as long as she lived.

I had now finished at Nanny Frisby's school, and not old enough to go to Mr. Gattlief's, at Witham on the Hill, a distance of two miles and a half. My father said there would be many things he could put me to, such as plough driving, pulling up weeds, keeping the birds from the corn, and many other jobs too numerous to write down.

I remember I was sent to keep the birds from taking a field of peas. I had to be up in the morning by five o'clock, and was forbidden to leave before eight at night. I was one evening so exhausted that I laid myself down and slept until eleven o'clock. My mother became alarmed, and one half of the

Parish were out looking for me, and it was only by their loud calling that I was woke up; but my father being very severe I was obliged to keep to the job.

CHAPTER II.

SCHOOL DAYS.

So time passed on until I was about ten years old. As I had not received any education since I left Nanny Frisby, except what my father had taught me on Sunday and winter evenings, it was agreed that I should go with William Swingler, (who was my chief companion at play, except my eldest brother,) to Mr. Gattlief, at Witham-on-the-Hill, as often as I could be spared, at least when there was nothing particular for me to do at home. Little Bytham could not boast of any other school, but Nanny Frisby's, except a dancing school, as about that time a Mr. Monk, styled himself a dancing master, came and hired a room at the Green Man Public House, to give lessons one afternoon in a fortnight to any young or old persons who might honor him with their company. Where he came from I do not know, all I know is, that he was such a peculiar looking man, and riding such a poor little half-starved pony, with, as I was, told five or six large handkerchieves tied round his neck, so that we could only see his eyes as he rode into the village. As we knew his time we did as often as possible meet at the door of the Green Man, where we also saw his pupils step in, which I named Mr. Monk's dancing dogs, for which I got myself very much disliked by the young ladies, although I married one of them after.

So on a Monday morning we started. As I said before it was two-and-a-half miles. Before we got half way there we were hungry, so we sat down and ate our dinners, then on to school. As we were young and fresh boys, we were told to take our seats on a long form or stool, where I sat all the time I went to the school, which was when I was about twelve years old. As we were going one morning, instead of going over a bridge, we agreed to walk over a willow tree, that had fallen across the brook, being rails on the opposite side, and I being first, Swingler gave me a push, and into the brook I went head foremost into about four feet of water, and being frightened lest I should be drowned, he did all in his power to get me out. After getting out and righting myself as well as I could, we had a jolly fight over it, in which I proved to be the best man. After that we went to school, not daring to go home as I was, with all my clothes wet. It was not found out by my parents before Sunday; as I changed my linen then, I had to give a full account of the matter. Things went on about the same, and I began to be quite tired of school, as I was not put to writing, ciphering, or grammar, Mr. Gattlief wishing to take an inn or Public house, it seemed not his study to improve the ideas of his young scholars, but we were very often most severely punished. When Mr. G. had cause to leave the school, which he very often did, he gave orders to one of the elder boys, to put down the name of any boy that might misbehave during his absence, on a slate, and as the elder boys liked or at least seemed to glory in seeing the younger ones punished, on his return he was sure to find several of our names down, and frequently without any cause. My name was frequently amongst those to be administered for punishment by a strong ash plant across our thighs, as we sat on the long stool, as hard as he could strike and for several strokes. Some times after that he would come and strike our hands with a flat rule. This went on until I dreaded to go to the school and I made up my mind not to go any more, as I had no companion. It wanted about six weeks to harvest, and I resolved spend my time about in the fields, at least play the truant.

On the Friday as my father was returning from Stamford market, he espied me and Swingler playing in a field: William S. was keeping birds from the corn. Before he came to us, and not knowing that he had seen me, I crawled into a bed of nettles in a ditch bottom ; he came to me and called, I then thought he had seen me : I shewed myself from my hiding place, and he made me go with him and gave me a severe flogging.

Next morning he seemed to be more in a hurry than usual for me to go to school ; I was to have my breakfast and go off at once, which I did. On my way, and about half a mile from home, I joined Bill Swingler (as he was usually called), we were walking by a hedge side towards a stone pit, agreeing to build a house during that day; at that time my father struck me a sharp blow right across my shoulders with an ash plant, he getting up to us unnoticed, by either of us. The blow was so sharp, I darted off at the moment, he following and telling me to stop. I told him if I did I should be late for school, knowing if he caught hold of me he would severely punish me. Finding I was running faster than he could, he turned back and went home, and sent my eldest brother over to Witham-on-the-Hill to see if I was at school, and ask Mr. Gattlief how long I had been absent. I was not there Mr. G. said, and had not been for six weeks. As my brother returned I met him, and asked him where he had been.

He told me and said what a bad boy I was, and he should tell the truth to my father. I tried to pursuade him not, but my entreaties were useless. We walked home together, and my father being at home, I was ordered into an outer barn, stripped of all my clothes, even my shirt I had to take off, and with a ground ash—and no one dare come to take my part—I was so cut and punished that my back was a long time before it healed and got well, that being on the Saturday. On the Monday morning I was sent to fetch my books, which only comprised a testament and a spelling book. I much dreaded the job, but was obliged to go. When I got to the school, Mr. Gattlief and his wife were at breakfast, and between the door and the seat I always sat upon—and no other in the school, as they had broken up on the Saturday for harvest—I said, Good morning, Sir. He said, Good morning to you Sir; I am glad to see you. Sit down; when I have finished my breakfast I will pay you for not coming the last six weeks. I said, If you please, Sir, I am come for my books : I hope you will not flog me, as my father did that on Saturday. No reply to that; but I saw by his looks he intended to do so. He soon rose from his seat, and went to his desk and looked over his old stock of canes, but I suppose he thought none of them good enough for the job. He then passed me and went into an out-house, where I knew his canes were kept. The moment he got in the closet, I having my eye on my books, which were lying on a rack above my head, I stepped upon the stool, took my books, passed Mrs. Gattlief, took up my hat which I had laid close to the door, and as that was already open, I was out and running down the street at my best pace, when I heard my master calling out to the people to stop me, instead of which, one and all of them said, run

C

boy, you will beat him. Some said, go on boy, he can't catch you : you'll beat him. So we ran through the village, which is about a quarter of a mile long, when he gave up the chase. His last words were, in a loud tone, " I will pay you out for it some day." But thanks to Goodness, that day has never come, as that was the end of my schooling, except what my father taught me at home.

As harvest was close at hand, I had to settle down to business : was up at four o'clock in the morning, and seldom in to supper before nine at night, taking any work that I was able to do at that time.

My father was asked by Lady Willoughby's agent if he would undertake to sell the venison that was not wanted to be given away, as well as the offals of the deer; as they had at that time as Mr. Scoles told me, 1500 head of bucks and does in the park, besides about 50 stags and hinds; consequently, there would be a great deal of offal to dispose of. My father accepted the offer and put the business into my hands, which pleased me much, as the sale of it occupied me three or four days a week during the buck and doe season. I could bring home from ten to fifteen shillings a day, which pleased me much better than going to work in the harvest field. So time passed on for about two years.

I now being fourteen years old, my father applied for the rabbits killed on her Ladyship's estate, as well as those from General Johnstone's of Witham-on-the-Hill, and General Reynordson's of Holywell, and obtained them ; and there being a large quantity, I found we required a better horse, which my father refused to buy.

As I wanted to do all the marketing, and finding my father took a little more drink than did him good, (for he took but little when at home and was always looked upon as a steady man, which he was,) I was now at my wits end to get a suitable nag. Having seen men and women about the streets in Stamford selling mushrooms, and this the end of harvest being the season for them, I made up my mind to do all I could in that line. The first week I gathered as many as brought me in twenty-one shillings. In carrying on this trade I gathered as many as I could on one day, and on the next carried them in baskets on my arm to Stamford, a dis-tance of eight miles, (sixteen there and back) besides walking about the town, and then doing other work after I got home, was almost enough to make one tired.

After a few weeks I began to look out for a horse. Stand-ing one day close to the Boat Inn, Stamford, I heard one man tell another that Mr. Baxter wanted to sell poor old Ranter, and from what I heard I thought it would suit us. I asked further about him, and they said he was one of the best in Stamford, but had lately gone blind; nevertheless, as he was near thorough-bred, and only seven years old, he would do a great deal of work, for they had known him for four years. I had reason to believe the truthfulness of their statement, as I knew them very well. I went at once to see Mr. Baxter, who was a blacksmith and farrier, living near to the George Hotel, St. Martin's. He happened to be at home. I said, " I understand, Sir, you have got a horse which you wish to sell? " He said, " I have, my boy; who wants one?" I said, " I do, Sir." " Who are you? " I said, " My name is Dale, from Little Bytham," and then asked the price of it. " Well," he said, " You had better go and look at him : he is in a paddock just outside the town; my man shall go with you, and when you have seen him we will talk about the

c2

price." I went and saw the horse, and liked the appearance of him very much; and from the character I heard of him, I made up my mind to purchase him. I went back and told the gentleman I thought the horse would suit if the price was not too much. He said, " Well, to some I should ask ten pounds; but I like the looks of you, and if you like him at seven pounds ten shillings, you shall have him." I said, " I have not got money enough with me, but I think I can borrow as much as I want." He asked me whether I knew any one in Stamford. I told him I had an uncle named Mr. Farrant. " O, " he said, " then you will borrow the money of him?" I said, " No, I should borrow what I wanted of Mr. Watson, foreman for Messrs Stevenson the tanners." So he said I could have the horse when I took him the money.

I found Mr. Watson at home having tea. I told him my business, and he lent me the money, at the same time telling me that he knew the horse to be a very good one, and that it would be cheap if I could get him for the money. I told him he should have the money on the following Friday; and returning to Mr. Baxter, was very pleased to ride him home without a saddle.

My father made no objections, as I promised to pay on Friday. Well, on that day I went to my bank early; for whatever money I saved, I put into a hole in a very old stone wall at the end of our village. Before I adopted this plan, as soon as any of my family knew that I had money in my pocket, they would borrow it, and I very seldom saw it again; so I took a stone out of the wall, and made a hole in the mortar in the centre thereof, put in my money as I got it together, and replaced the stone. I seldom went to my money by daylight, neither did I ever loose any of it. I passed the old wall and pointed it out to my present wife, and Mr. Lintott, a friend of mine, about six weeks from the time of my writing this, as we were then staying at Bytham for a few days.

According to promise I went and paid Mr. Watson the money I had borrowed of him to pay for my horse, and was now ready for the rabbit and venison season, which commencd in November.

Soon after I bought the horse, my father was going down to Spalding. The way he went by Market Deeping toll-gate and down Littleworth Drove was twenty-four miles. I told him the night before that I should like to go with him, when he replied that he should ride the horse and not drive, and therefore I should not be able to go. I told him I should go, if I walked. He said it would be forty-eight miles, and he intended starting at four o'clock in the morning, and that I had much better stay at home. I said I want to know Spalding. Being determined to go, I listened to hear him get up, which he did at three o'clock, and was off at four. I was ready, and started after him, keeping sight of him by star-light, sometimes being compelled to run at a brisk pace, for he was a sharp rider, and wished to be there very early. When we got within about five miles of the town, he saw me and asked if I should like to ride. I said, " If you please," thinking he would alight, and let me mount the saddle ; instead of which, he told me to climb a gate by the road-side and take my seat on the horse behind. I did so for about a hundred yards, and then slipped off, saying I thought he was plenty for the poor horse to carry, and I should walk, which I did the rest of the day, not being invited again to ride. I did not sit down more than one hour during the day, and as we did not get home until eight at night, of course I felt a little tired, yet did not complain, knowing that I was soon to have the horse and marketings to myself.

I attended the markets for four winters, up to the age of eighteen, at the end of which time I left my father and mother, never more to sleep under their roof, and I do not think I even took a meal at their expense ever afterwards. I left home with one half-crown in my pocket, and emptying my bank, I made my wardrobe a little comfortable, but not complete. After I left, poor old ranter was sold, my youngest brother took my place with another horse; but they soon went wrong. I had done wonders with poor old ranter, and never knew him to fail but once. I always fed him well if I went short of refreshment myself. I have left home for Sleaford for the Monday's market at three o'clock in the morning, being obliged to be there early, and could not go beyond a walking pace on account of having a load, and I have not been home before seven at night, and a half-a-pint of ale with a penny roll is all I have had. My father allowed my dinner, but if I did not have it the money went into my bank. It was my duty to look after and feed my horse, as he had four journeys a week from November to February viz., Sleaford on Monday, Spalding on Tuesday, either of which was forty-eight miles there and back; Falkingham on Thursday, there and back only thirty two miles; Stamford on Friday, which was only sixteen miles. Grantham was thirty-two. On my returning, I could ride or drive a sharp pace, as few horses could go before poor old ranter.

In summer-time he had rest, but little fell to my lot, as a great deal of my time was taken up with Squire Hopkinson of Careby, who occupied four large farms, lying several miles apart. He chose to have me with him, and I was very fond of his company, for he was one of the best judges of stock and farming of his day, and he always paid me well, besides finding me a good nag. He lived to a good old age, and at his death he left ten thousand pounds to each of his seven daughters. He used to buy and graze the large bay Yorkshire horses, those suitable for gentlemen's carriages. He never put more than one in a field, and a donkey with each. He kept several donkeys, for they were the best companions for young horses, as they will neither race nor injure the horse, so that he will get fat all the quicker.

About this time he gave one to Mr. Sculthorpe, a gentleman who married his third daughter, and lived at Warmington, about eighteen miles from Caveby. The horse was five years old, a bright bay, and a very fine one, just out of the breaker's hands. One day they put him in the team to plough, and on the next he was put in the gig to run Mrs. Sculthorpe and daughter down to Caveby to spend a week. After a few days' rest I was sent for to drive Mrs. Sculthorpe and Miss Lucy Hopkinson to Stamford, thinking I was a better whip than his groom although he was much older than myself. The ladies said they had every confidence; and I have no doubt everthing would have been satisfactory had they not interfered, but when we reached the top of Pole Street, which is about half-a-mile straight run to the bottom of High Street, with a descent, the ladies said, " Let him go, Nathaniel; let us cut a dash and shine through the town." I touched him with the whip, which I had not done before, and away we went full trot to the bottom of High Street, and turning into St. John's we were all but over on my side, and near as possible into a silver-smith's large bay window. I threw myself across the ladies which brought the near wheel to the ground, the horse

still going at full trot   In the middle of St. John's street a
dog came out of a baker's shop, and ran at his heels, which
frightened him into a galop.   I turned into St. Mary's street,
when I saw the Marquis of Exeter's carriage coming, and not
far from us.   I pulled on the near side to make way, the near
wheel caught the curve stone, and over we went.   I held to
the reins until the stone cut through my coat, and the people
calling out to me to let go.   Mr. Simpson and his men were
looking out of the "George and Angel Yard," surrounded
the horse, and forced him up the steps of St. Mary's Church,
which cut both his knees and broke the Gig.

As soon as I had directed the ladies to be taken in a sedan
chair to a lawyer's, a cousin of theirs, I sent the horse to my
old friend Baxter's, of whom I bought poor Ranter.   The
gig I sent to Spencer's the coachmaker in High Street, and
gave each party orders to do the best they could, which they
did.   I then went to see how the ladies were, and found them
very much bruised and plastered about their faces, and the
doctor with them.   After lunch I ordered a chaise and pair,
and asked the lawyer to go home with us, which he did, and
satisfied the old Squire that it was not our fault, but the fault
of the dog : so the Squire gave orders that the owner of the
dog should be prosecuted.   The lawyer was to commence with
an action at once.   He said he would, but never intended to
do so.

All passed off well : the ladies were put to bed and soon
got over it.   On Friday the Stamford newspaper came out
with the account headed "furious driving," but the poor old
Squire did not believe it, so it all passed over.

When I was about eleven years of age, General Birch
Reynardson of Holywell Hall sent to know if my father

would let me go to Stamford to fetch some parcels and letters. I rode a donkey at that time; so my donkey and I started and got to Holywell about mid-day, and rode up to the front door. The General, Mrs. Reynardson, and the daughters were at the front window looking out for me. The General came out and said I was a good boy, but I ought to have went to the stables. I told him I did not know the way. So he took me and my donkey to the stables, and told the groom to feed him; and then introduced me to the housekeeper, and told her to do the same to me. After that, I was to go back to Stamford for other things, which I did, and got home at six o'clock at night. Not a bad days work for a donkey—in all, thirty-two miles, having only one feed.

At that time we had fourteen weeks frost, with a great fall of snow. I remember much snow fell on the Thursday night, as the farmers were obliged the next morning to set all the men they could get to cut a road through the snow upon Hornby Heath before they could get their teams to Stamford with corn. The snow lay fourteen feet thick for a long distance, as it had been snowing and drifting for a long time. After two or three nights sharp frost we could walk across the fields over hedges and ditches for miles. I have not seen anything like it since.

I think it was the following harvest that we had a total eclipse of the sun : we were in the field, and about five o'clock in the afternoon it got quite dusk, and not knowing anything about the eclipse, we were astonished to hear the fowls going to roost. Rooks, and all the birds seemed to be quiet for the night. When on our way home, to our surprise, the sun again made its appearance, and we had to go back to work.

The next harvest after having bought the blind horse, my

D

two brothers and I were reaping wheat near to the boundary hedge of Little Bytham and Witham-on-the-Hill, in which there were several rabbits. My father was with us about four o'clock in the afternoon, when one of my brothers looking up, saw the Rev. William Hopkinson seated in the top of a tree, waiting for the young rabbits to come out so that he might shoot them. He was full six miles from home, but how he got there we could not tell. My brother laughed and pointed to the parson so that he might cause us to look. My father saw him in an instant, and recognized him. He gave us a stern look, so we all went on with our work again, and dare not look up any more at the Reverend Gentleman.

It happened soon afterwards that I turned my blind horse out to graze on a piece of waste land by the side of a brook, and near to a house occupied by two old bachelors; at least, they were about fifty. They were tall stout men, occupying a little land, and kept two horses, which they frequently turned on this said piece of waste-land. They were afraid my horse would rob theirs of a bit of grass, as they were always called greedy, although they had plenty of money, so James came to tell me if I did not take my horse away he should take him to the pound, as he would not have him staring in their window. I said, you booby, he is blind, and cannot see in your window.

The first time he met me in the village he came behind me and caught me by both ears, lifted me up, and lugged me until the blood began to run. Mr. Rudkin, a farmer, came up and caused him to let me down. As he was constable he went and told my father how ill I had been used by Stanhope; and advised my father to go over to the Rev. William Hopkinson and get a summons, and he would go with us as a witness; so my father took me and obtained a summons. A few days afterwards we all went to Morton—to the study of Mr. Hopkinson, who said to Stanhope, "Well, Sir, how came you to ill use this boy in the manner you did. What was the cause?" He said, "Because he called me a booby." Mr. Hopkinson said, "I do not wonder at it." After hearing the evidence of Mr. Rudkin, Stanhope was about to say something more, but Mr. H. stopped him, and said, "I have known Mr. Dale for many years, and do not wish to meet with a more respectable man, and from what I saw last harvest, his sons were well trained." He made Stanhope pay a fine and expenses, which caused him to go off grumbling.

About this time we had a very wet harvest. I have not witnessed one like it since. A great deal of the wheat shot out green from the ear before it was cut; and as my father was afraid we should not have any good seed, he set all of us to pick out all the sound and best ears, and to keep them by themselves.

After harvest it was thrashed out, and as we were dividing the chaff from the wheat with a fan, Squire Hopkinson rode up to the barn door and asked to look at the sample. After he had looked at it, he said he would take all we had to spare, and asked the price. My father said he did not know, as he was not at Stamford market the Friday before. So the Squire said I will give you one guinea per bushel, and take all you have like this.

When our first batch of bread of that harvest came from the bake-house, we ate it out of the tins it was baked in with a spoon.

That year, the harvest was not all gathered in until the next February. We were cutting beans in the middle of November.

D2

That year I was sent to Stamford for hops and salt : the hops were five shillings per pound, the salt was five shillings per stone, and the best wheaten flour was seven shillings and sixpence per stone, but not any really good. All the poor people at that time ate barley bread, and barley flour was five shillings per stone

When I was about sixteen years old I went to visit my aunt Claypole of Asalackby, my uncle having died a short time previous to my visit. My cousin John, who was eighteen years old, was not enough of a farmer to manage and carry things out agreeably to my aunt's wishes, therefore she had engaged her nephew Richard Dale, as her bailiff; he well knowing how business should be done, but too lazy to do much himself, although in the prime of life. During my stay, a field was in good order that was to be sown with oats. The morning being windy my aunt wished Richard to sow them, thinking he would do them better than the man, as at that time almost all corn was sown broad-cast. We all started to the field with the horses, and the harrows and seed in the cart. When Richard had been round once, he said the wind was so strong that it made the sowing hard work. So he said to the middle man, who was about sixteen years old, " Tom, boy, put smiler to the cart, then I can stand on the hind part of it and sow very well. It will be easier than walking." All was done according to order. Hopper filled, and Richard all right. He said, " Gee-O, boy, go on." The mare moved, and out came Richard, heels over head. He said, " Halloo, boy, this wont do, I am down. Pick up the oats, and we'll try another scheme." So he did, by mounting one of the horses backwards. Hopper filled again, and set upon the horse's hind part of the back. Said he, " All right now, boy, Gee-O, go on." He did, and Richard was quickly on the ground, for the moment he moved his arms to sow, down he came and got a tremendous fall; so bad that he could not sow the oats at all that day. On our way home we were all forbid to say a word about the bit of business, but he had not been in the house many minutes before he told all about it, for which he was laughed at as long as he lived, and that was for many years after.

About that time my aunt lost about one hundred very fine sheep, through a dog in a state of madness. He passed through several of her fields, biting many; and as it was for several days before they knew that the dog was mad, and before they noticed the sheep to froth at the mouth, a deal of mischief was done. They gave them drinks from Doctor Beecham of Bourne, which seemed to have the desired effect as a preventative. Several of the farmers in the neighbourhood suffered much from the same dog until he was shot. He was a well-bred pointer.

I one day came home from plough wet through with rain, and before I entered the door of the house, I looked into an out-house, where I saw the the woodden coal-scoop on fire, being started by some live coals that were put into it. A child's chair made of hosiers that was close to it was in flames The loft above was full of old loose hay, stored away for the next winter. Fortunately there was a pail of water standing outside the door, which I at once threw on the flames and put them out. Another five minutes, and all must have been burnt down, as the houses and out-houses were all old and thatched.

My father did a great deal of business in the wool trade at that time, and executed some very large orders. I have been from home as much as six weeks at a time, buying, taking up, and packing, which made me understand the nature of wool, which I was very fond of being amongst.

One harvest my eldest brother and I went and cut a field of wheat containing twenty acres in twenty-one days. I was then sixteen, and my brother was a year-and-a-half older. It was valued, and said to be worth twelve shillings per acre cutting, as all of it was cut with a sickle and hook. I cut with the latter.

The following harvest, Mr. Richard Niel of Creeton, offered to back us two to cut one acre for neatness, against any two men in his village; but they dare not take the bet.

CHAPTER III.

AT GRIMSTHORPE.

In 1823, I was called to Grimsthorpe by the Right Honourable Lady Willoughby de Ersby, to assist Mr. Scoles, who was
park keeper and bailiff. The steward, Mr. Clutton, lived in
Essex, and only came to Grimsthorpe twice a year, to secure
the rents and to look over our accounts.

I had not been there long before I was surcharged. I had
leave to carry a gun and shoot, and was charged with killing
game before I could get my license. I was summoned to meet
the magistrates, amongst whom were Mr. Migley, and Mr.
Hopkinson in the chair. I was called in, and the surveyor
handed a book to me, and said, " Have you within the last six
months killed a head of game with your gun ?" I said, "No,
Sir." Mr. Hopkinson said, " I told you so." Then he said
to me, " You can go, Dale." Had Mr. Surveyor put the
question in a different form, I must have pleaded guilty; as
it was the shot that killed the game, and not the gun. I saw
the creep-hole as soon as the words passed from his lips. Of
course, it was not for me to tell him what to say.

As we kept the fine old sort of blood-hounds, Mr. Scoles and
I were invited to Lord Clifford's of Ernham to try to kill a fat
out-lying buck.   We started about three o'clock in the morning, and was all ready for the hunt by four, when we tried
the hounds round the wood where he had been seen the night
before.   They were soon on his scent, and away they went,
making the woods ring with their loud musical tone.   Both
of us alighted from our horses, and took our stand at a little
distance from each other, when he came by me within about
fifty yards.   I then shot, lost sight of him, but soon heard a
groan and scuffle in the wood.   I ran in, and there he laid
dead.   The dogs soon came up, I let them have the blood, and
then gave the "death holla," when the other parties soon
came up to the spot.   His lordship was so delighted, and he
was the finest buck I ever saw.   Each haunch weighed thirty-
two pounds.   We then took him home, and very much enjoyed
ourselves afterwards.

Just before Lord Gwyder died he was very much annoyed by
the lady's maids and vallets going about the walks after supper.   He said he could hear their noise as he sat in the drawing
room; so he told Mr. Scoles he would have something done to
stop it; and suggested that Mr. S. should have several pounds
of gunpowder, and lay trains up and about the walks, all leading to one point; and when the girls and valets had got well
away, to set fire to the starting point.   It was done, and a fine
game we had: girls fainted, and the valets had quite a job to
protect and get them away.   It had the desired effect, and
they never knew the principal actor.

One day in December, we had Mr. Herring to assist us, as
he lived at a house in the park, about a mile from ours.   Going
home about Ten o'clock at night, his horse refused to go forward,

and began to back. He heard a squeaking on the ground, and getting off his horse, found it was a drove of rats coming from his lodge to ours.

The Right Hon. Lindsey Burril received a letter one day in November from a gentleman to inform him that there were a great many snipes in Cowbit Wash near Spalding. He sent to say he should like Mr. Scoles, Mr. Chapman, and myself to go with him. Next morning as we were riding sharp to the castle, Mr. Scoles' horse slipped up, and its rider in falling to the ground put out his shoulder. He however re-mounted, and on we went to a distance of twenty miles, yet did not see a single snipe. When we started from the inn where we left our horses, the Hon. Lindsey Burril said that he and I would go together, and Mr. Chaplin with Mr. Scoles. We waded through the fen dykes, and the first we came to was about four feet of water. The Hon. Lindsey being six feet three in height, said I had better go first, he keeping hold of my collar, and if he found it too deep he would pull me back. However the water did not come higher than my chin, and when we got out we had a sup of brandy.

On we went until we got tired of the thing, as there were no snipes to be seen. We called the other two back, fetched our horses, and rode to Thorney. There we killed four. Reaching Peterborough, we bought dry clothes, had dinner, and went home, having rode about forty miles for four snipes.

A few days after we went to shoot in a wood near to Bourne. As soon as we let our dogs go, several of them got caught in snares. Mr. Scoles and the other gentlemen went to another wood, while I went to the keeper's house to fetch him. I rode sharp, found him at home, took him up behind me, and rode back to the wood as quickly as possible. The snares I had seen were gone. As the men were taking them up we went up to

E

them, and after having a sharp fight, marched them down to Bourne, about two miles off, and gave them into the constable's hands, who locked them up.   The people in Bourne were surprised to see three of their own townsmen who had said they would not be taken by any body, marched into Bourne by us two. Lady Willoughby's doctor came to ask if I wanted any help. I said, "No thank you ; they will soon be in the lock up."   Next morning they were brought before the Rev. W. Hopkinson, who committed them to prison ; so we finished with them.

Soon after they came out of prison, I happened to be at Bourne Fair.   About eleven at night I was met by a friend, who said he had seen an old sweet-heart of his, and promised to meet her and have a dance.   If I would go with him, as he would not stop long, we could ride home together.   I went with him, but soon found we were getting into a bad quarter. He said, "Don't be afraid, all's right."   So on we went.   I heard the fiddle as we found our way up a kind of a passage about fifteen yards from the road.   My neighbour Thomas Sharp led the way.   By chance one of the poachers was stand- ing in the door-way, who, as soon as he saw me, shut to the door and fastened it.   Sharp, in forcing his knee against it, broke the fastening, and in we went.   The fiddle ceased to play, and soon a fight commenced.   My friend fetched his man down, the blood flew about, and his opponent dare not meet him again. The two others caught hold of me, dragged me down the passage, and were going to put me into a fen dyke with about two feet of water and as much mud, about twenty yards from the house.   As we were getting near the ditch, finding they kept my friend back, I instantly sprung forward, faced them, and putting my hand to my breast pocket, said, "The first man that touches me I will blow him through."   They supposed I had got a pistol; but however, I had not, nor any other weapon about me, except the spurs on my boots. I turned and went into the house, and found my companion all-right in the hands of the old sweetheart, who said he should not be hurt by any of them. I dared those inside as I had said to the two that dragged me out. They evidently were afraid and proffered to treat us with ale, which we refused. The ladies then said we should take a cup of tea with them, that we accepted, after that we departed in peace; but it was a lesson which had a lasting impression, and I never did the like again.

As I could run well I was frequently invited out to take poachers. I once had a strong fight with rook stealers. As there is a fine rookery on each side of the castle, and the keepers had watched them day and night until they thought them able to fly and take care of themselves. As Mr. Scoles always gave three days for shooting, to the tenants, farmers, and tradespeople from Stamford, Bourne, and other Neighbourhoods, we could kill hundreds of dozens, as we had usually twelve or fifteen guns each day. But at the time I am about to write, the Right Honourable Lindsey Burril was there on a visit, and wishing to have a little shooting as soon as they could fly well. The two under keepers whose business it was to look after them, were gone away from home for a day's holiday. I was sent for by the Honourable Lindsey Burril to the castle on other business. After I left him in his room, I went into the butler's pantry to take a glass of ale and a crust of bread and cheese, from there I went to the stables, took my horse, and was going to the park, when I saw by the manner of the old rooks, that there was something going on wrong. Knowing the keepers were away from home, I went to see the cause, and found two men, named Charles Maxey and John Holmes. Maxey was up at the

E2

top of one of the trees, taking and knocking down those that could not fly. I told the men they were doing wrong, but if they would walk off, I said I wonld not expose them. However Máxey said he would not come down until he got and killed all he could ; bnt with throwing some stones at him, he very soon changed his mind, and came down. Then a scuffle for the rooks which Holmes had got in his possession. In the scuffle, the rooks were pulled limb from limb. Maxey then wished to fight, and struck me a blow. I thought I had better not, being alone, and each of them taller and somewhat heavier than myself, (as at that time I weighed 11½ stones. and was never more than five feet five inches high). I was twenty-one, Maxey forty, and Holmes about nineteen years old.

Before we parted, Mr. Scoles came riding up, and wanted to know what was amiss. So I told him all what had occured. He said they should be summonsed ; but I not liking the blow I had received from Maxey—he being hot with fight and in a rage—said, " We will have no summons ; we will settle it now you are here to see fair play." So he leaped from his horse, there being then a backer for each, we set to work. The first twenty minutes I found I had got a job before me, as he was not only a stone mason, but almost as hard as stone itself. I hit and got away, and stuck to his wind and ribs until I broke two of them for him. He was then led to his sister's house in Grimsthorpe where they put him to bed, but he did not get home for some days. I then went to the castle and told the Hon. Lindsey Burril. He said he was sorry he was not there. As he was six feet three inches in height, with good science, and about forty-five years of age he might have stopped the fight ; but as I only got a black eye, he was very pleased.

One night the keepers asked me if I would go with them to watch the rooks in the groves, as they thought a party was coming to steal the young ones. I at once consented, and we had not been long there before we heard a boy say to his father, " Dang yah, Dad ; what a liar yah are. Yah said they were all fligged-flyers, and they are all bare-bolshers." We soon surprised them and sent them away without the " bolshers."

The late Hon. Peter Drummond Burrel one day had company at Grimsthorpe, and after dinner when the servants were clearing away, the footman and under butler as soon they came out of the dining room met me and began to show some sleight-of-hand tricks, when the butler dropped the tray on the floor in the passage, breaking some of the dinner service. The crash was heard in the dining room, but there was not anything said. As they were picking up the broken pots the footman said, " Never mind, Peter pays for all." The next day the butler asked his master what coloured dinner service he would like. The master replied, " The same as yesterday." But contrary to order, another coloured service was put on. When the Honourable entered the room he enquired why his order was not obeyed. They told him it was a mistake. He said, " Never mind, Peter pays for all." However, it passed off with a caution.

The late Rowland Hill's cook once asked the footman to fetch the milk for breakfast, it being a very wet morning the boy had not come. The footman said it was not his work, the coachman might go. The coachman refused. The cook then went and told Mr. Hill, when he ordered the carriage directly. The carriage was soon at the door; the servants all wondering, until Mr. Hill, with can in hand, entered the carriage, bidding the footman to mount the box in full dress, and the coachman to drive for the milk. The milk was fetched, and the carriage had to be cleaned. This stayed all further complaints about fetching the milk. I heard it from Mr. Hill when on a visit in the country.

About this time Mr. Scole's brother and I were spending an evening at the castle. About eleven o'clock we started home, Mr. Scole's groom was going home at the same time. I told him to let Mr. Charles Scoles ride his horse and he could get up and ride behind me, which he did; but it so annoyed him, that when he had rode about half-a-mile, he took me by both hands and threw me from my horse, and at the time hurt me very much: the wind was knocked out of me, and the horse gone away into the park by itself. I lay on the ground, and heard Mr. Scoles say to the man, " You fool, John; you might have killed him; you deserve punishing." After I had recovered I rose from the ground, and gave the fellow a box of the ear. He then showed fight, and struck me in return. This led to a fight by moonlight; Mr. Scoles seeing fair play. In about ten minutes I finished him off by giving him some sharp cuts on the face. We went home and went to bed. Next morning he got out of bed and looked in the glass, and seeing his face was cut very much, he took one of the horses and rode to Bourne, a distance of five miles, to Doctor Simpson, Lady Willoughby's doctor. After telling him how it was done, and to make the most of it, covered his face all over with stripes of white sticking plaster. When he returned we could just see his mouth and eyes. After a lecture from Mr. Scoles we finished this job.

As it was Lady Willoghby's wish to give the trrdespeople at Stamford a little venison at Christmas, I was sent with it, a distance of twelve miles. As well as venison, I took each a nice bunch of misletoe, as a large quantity grew on the fine old thorn-bushes in the park, so much so the keepers were obliged to watch all night to prevent it being cut and carried away in carts.

Charles Scoles and Thomas Bywaters, one of the under keepers, wished to go with me, and as I was driving in a light spring-cart, I consented to take them. We finished our evening at Mr. Monk's the gun-smith. About twelve o'clock at night the hostler came to say he wished to lock up, and if we wanted our horse we must go with him, which we agreed to do. I carried a bag of shot, and asked the hostler to take another, as each of the other gentlemen refused to carry it. As we passed through Red Lion Square, Bywaters struck the hostler with the whip, as he had that in his hand. The man complained, and I remonstrated with him, when he then struck me. I threw the bag of shot into his neck-hole, sent him head foremost on to the ground. After that he was quiet. As we passed through St. Mary's Street, Scoles took a basket out of the hands of a child who was walking the street at the time; the child began to cry, and went home and told her father; so that by the time we got to the inn, the child with her father, police, and a drove of people came after us. The girl pointed the man out that took her basket, and whilst they were parleying over the matter, Bywaters and I got out back way into our cart, and I drove away sharp. Scoles telling the people that it was Bywaters and not him that had taken the basket. The police followed us. I saw them coming, and I drove sharp, and turning out of one street, Bywaters caught the rein, thinking I was passing the turning, pulled the near wheel on to the corner of a house, and over we went, cart as well. We lifted up the cart, put in the bags of shot and was off in an instant, just as one man laid his hand on the back part of the cart. I gave him a sharp rap of the knuckles, struck the horse, and in an instant we were in a sharp gallop, leaving all behind. They put Scoles in the lock-up but he was bailed out about two o'clock on Sunday morning to appear before the Mayor on Monday morning. He was set at liberty by paying a small fine, and came home with a black eye, which was a lesson not forgotten by him ever afterwards.

Soon after this we were shooting rabbits in Car Wood. My father drove to us to take them away, and my youngest brother who was then about five years old, wished to go with him. My mother at first objected to his going but at last she consented, as the child was very fond of me and wished to be with me. My father had alighted from the cart, and left the child in, thinking he would be safer there. When only a few yards from him, the mare looked round and saw a donkey and cart standing on the other side, with which the men had taken the nets to the wood in. She started off at full speed,—the child jumped out,—the wheel passed over his body,—and he was dead in a short time. I was not more than four hundred yards off, and hearing the child and my father calling me, I ran as quickly as possible ; but before I got up, life was extinct. Mr. Scoles tried to let blood from the arms, but to no purpose. All was over with the poor dear, a pet with us all, and the youngest of eleven children. My readers will judge the grief of my poor mother when the child was taken home. I had sent a person on to break the shock, but it was very great. It was the will of the Almighty, and for the child's good, and therefore we ought not to grieve.

As I was one day riding across the park, in the month of

October, I passed the herd of hinds, which the master stag was keeping charge over, as in the rutting season they always keep the hinds close together during the day, as a dog would do a flock of sheep. When the master stag becomes exhausted and weak, then the next master stag comes up and beats him off, keeping the hinds together; neither will he let one of them leave the herd, for if any one attempts to do such a thing, he goes at her and fetches her back as a dog would a sheep. I suppose I was riding closer than he liked, being about sixty yards off, and passing at a walking pace, when I saw him at once spring towards me. I faced him, and discharged one barrel of shot at him. He stopped, shook his head, and quietly returned to his female companions.

As I have before said, my grand-father was bailiff for Squire Reynardson of Holywell Hall; and having occasion to cross the park, and not knowing the nature of the stag, he went too close, and in being attacked, was obliged to take protection from a large oak tree, walking round it as the stag moved, watching for more than an hour. At last the fellow saw another stag going towards the hinds, when he was induced to leave my grand-father, to go and turn back his rival, and in this way my grand-father escaped.

Mr. Scoles and I were riding through the park one Sunday morning, we passed the stags on our right hand, and some two-year-old colts on our left. We had been to speak to one of the keepers that lived at the gate on the Stamford or South side. Returning in about ten minutes, a stag had killed one of the horses by a stab in the heart, as if a ball had entered.

I had now been seven years under that excellent master Mr. Scoles, who had shown a lively interest in me, and had

F

afforded me every opportunity for improvement in farming, woods, plantations, game, deer, in short, everything that was carried on upon the estate; fishing as well, for we had all under our control.

At this time I was recommended to the Duke of Manchester by I. Fletcher, Esq., of Rushden Hall, Northamptonshire, and Alderman Gilchrist, of Stamford. The Duke coming home from Jamaica, where he had been Governor for twenty-one years; and on his return found many things contrary to his liking. Some of the land had been let from the home farm; the herd of deer, very small in number as well as in size, through being bred in and in, and not having a change of blood, as the Duke told me after, in the memory of man.

Game there was but little; but the place was smothered with rabbits, the woods eaten up and partly destroyed by them.

In July, 1828, I was applied to by the Duke; but the letter being delayed, and consequently, he not hearing from me so soon as he expected, he went to London and engaged a farmer's son, who was recommended to him in the name of Bishop, a fine young fellow, twenty-three years of age, and weighing fifteen stone. His father lived in Essex. Alderman Gilchrist told me he was very sorry, as the Duke was such a good master, and he should have liked for me to have had the situation.

Things passed on until October, when the Duke wrote for me to come up at once, as the young man did not suit that he had engaged. I rode up and saw the Duke, and he told me he would send Squire Fletcher to meet me at the stewards office to come to some arrangement the next morning. About nine o'clock in the evening he sent a gentleman to have some conversation with me as a sound, and he was to see the Duke the next morning at eight, and tell him what he thought to me in our conversation about business. The next morning he saw the Duke at the time appointed. The Duke said, " Well, have you seen this man?" The gentleman said, " Yes." " Well, what do you think to him?" He said, " Well, Your Grace, he is a little man." " Little be d——d," said the Duke. " I have tried the big ones, they are good for nothing, now I will try a little one; and from what I have heard of him, I shall have him." At nine o'clock I was sent for to the steward's office. Squire Fletcher was sent by the Duke to report and inform him what passed between the steward and me. As he was with the Duke the night before and heard the Duke tell him to engage me. Fletcher said nothing until I took my hat to walk off. I then heard him say to the steward, " It is all nonsense to let him go, as the Duke means to have him." When I went in the steward said, " Well, young man, you have come after this situation?" I said, " Yes, sir." On asking me what wages I required, I said " What perquisites does the Duke allow?" as I already knew by letter what my duties were to be. The steward said, " No perquisites; all you will have is a house to live in, firing, and rabbits for your own use." " Then I shall want so much wage." " No," the steward said, " I can get the Duke two men for that." I said, " Very well sir; and if I do come, who am I to look up to for orders?" He said, " Who do you expect?" I said, " The Duke, if I come; for I do not intend to have two masters," for I had heard that he had been master during the time the Duke had been away, and a hard one too, and I did not intend to be under him. If I went and did not suit, I could go back to

my old situation, as Lady Willoughby had said that it
should not be filled up until the expiration of six months,
as a brother of mine was to have it for that time. So after
this the steward said, " You are too independent, young man,
for Kimbolton." I said, " Very well, sir;" and with that
took up my hat, mounted my horse, and rode home.

I told Mr. Scoles and her Ladyship all about it, and they
said I had been too cheeky to the steward, and they felt sure
I should not go now. But however, when Mr. F. went and
told the Duke, he said, " That's the man I want;" and sent
for the steward, and gave him orders to write and tell me to
come on the tenth of November, and there would be a house
comfortably furnished for me to go to.

So I had to get my wardrobe together, visit, and say good-
bye to my friends at Grimsthorpe.

At the time I was staying at the castle, there was a quarrel
with Mr. Scoles and the french cook—Mr. Strappany. Her
Ladyship had given Mr. Scoles orders about some game, as
there was more in the larder than she would require, he could
take some away. Scoles walked into the larder, and was
taking down some of the game according to her Ladyship's
orders, when the cook saw him, came with his long knife, and
told Mr. Scoles he should not take any game out of his larder.
Mr. Scoles tried to explain the matter to him, but as the
french blood had got to boiling heat, he said to Mr. Scoles,
" You are a d——d thief; and if you dare to take another
hare down me vill stab you to the heart." Mr. Scoles having a
hare in his hand that had been paunched, and being on high
steps, hit the cook on both sides of the head and knocked him
down. The blood flew all over the cook's white cap with
tassel, white jacket, trousers, and apron. The cook then

sprang up and went down the cloister into her Ladyship's room, when the sight of him made her faint. The cook stood jabbering away, but long before he could be understood; but when he was, Mr. Scoles was sent for; it was then explained, and soon all made right.

CHAPTER IV.

AT KIMBOLTON.

On the 10th of November I came to live at Kimbolton. When I saw the Duke, he said I had better look round for the first fortnight, and he would tell a man to show me about. When the fornight had expired he sent for me, and asked if I thought I could settle at Kimbolton. I told him I could. He said, " We will now set to work. I intend to take more land to the Home Farm, and build a few more premises ; and in a few years I hope to build a new farm premises out of the park." He would also change his breed of sheep, which he did, to the " Dorsets ;" but not liking them, he tried the " Downs ;" and in a few years had a first-rate flock. He also changed his breed of beast, and took to the " Devons," and soon got a fine herd.

As I was desirous of having a finer lot of bucks and does, I wrote to Lord Willoughby de Ersby of Grimsthorpe, (his mother then being dead,) to ask him if he would give me a brace of bucks for a brace of ours. His reply was, " I have ordered my keeper to catch up two brace, and the first I shall give to the Duke, if he will except of them; and for the second I will take a brace of yours in exchange." I showed the letter to the Duke, and he was quite pleased. I soon set to work and caught ours, took them down to Grimsthorpe, and brought the two brace of fine bucks back, which the Duke was very pleased with.

After I had changed one brace with Lord Hardwick of Wimpole, Cambridgeshire; one brace with the Hon. Octavius Duncombe of Waresley Park; and one with the Duke of Bedford, Woburn Park; I bought ten does of the Late Lord Winchelsea; all of which I had to move from one park to the other.

With my favourite horse and dog, as both were well trained, I could go at any time between November and January and take three or four in two hours. I once took five for feeding in two hours and ten minutes, with one horse and one dog. The present Duke of Manchester and Lord Robert Montague witnessed it as well as others. Our deer were very strong, as we always fed them with beans, carrots, and hay, as much as they could eat. The Duke was very fond of his deer, and we increased the number to five hundred.

The Duke was fond of venison, and scarcely ever dined without it, dressed in some way or other. All the neighbouring gentlemen in and all round Kimbolton received a portion twice in the year, as the Duke told me it was not every gentleman that could keep deer; and by giving a little away it kept us on good terms with our neighbours. I used to give him venison nearly all the year round; so I used to stall about thirty to feed, and have a good many aveours, which I never valued at much. Spade does were fine, which I operated upon myself as well as the aveours. My dog always took them by the ear. The way I trained him to that, was by putting him on to a boar pig when about ten months old. Not too soon, or a bite from Mr. Pig might dishearten him.

Father, son, and grand-son, lasted me nineteen years without a mishap, either to dog or buck; but not so as regards myself. I had a bitch given to me by the late Duke of Bedford; she was fast, but she would not take hold. I was trying her one day, and she ran the buck down to the iron gates at the entrance to the castle, when the buck turned upon her. There we were for about fifteen minutes, before I could make Barber, who had got my dog "Sailor" in the Park, hear, the wind being wrong for the sound. When he did hear and let the dog go, he was soon with me. When I thought he had got the buck safe by the ear, I got off my horse, but the ear being cut short when a fawn, slipped from his teeth. I was in the act of running, thinking to throw him, when he came at me with such force, one antler in the bottom of my body, the other into my thigh, close to the pope's eye, but just to miss it, otherwise it would have been all up with me in a short time. Luckily, I saw him coming, and catching each horn in my hands, broke the force. It knocked me backwards, and there I lay fifteen minutes before my man came to take either dog or buck. I had the buck fast by the horns, and he all the time trying to stab me a second time, but I had strength to hold him back. I dare not let the dog come at him, fearing he might injure him. Several people were at a distance, but I dare not let them come to my assistance, for fear of the dog, which was watching me and the buck. The dog thinking it was hurting me, I had great difficulty in keeping him from the buck. At last, however, Barber came, and we made all-right. I was taken home and attended by Mr. Firnie, and in a month was quite well.

My horses I used to buy in about four years old, well-bred, and of as good a sort as I could meet with. My custom was

also to break and train them myself, as I have known many
a young horse spoilt by a breaker, and some few by bad
tempered grooms. In training, I always carried a few shgas
of oats, about six heads, cut off all the straws except one
which I wrap round the heads of a few of these little bundles
in my pocket. I had used to feed and coax my horse until he
would follow me any where. I had one which would jump the
fences when I was shooting, and follow me wherever I went.

When I bought a horse I never asked for a warranty, nor
did I ever give one. I sold one to young Mr. Islip of Milch-
bourn, I let him have it to try as he liked, and told him to
make all the enquiries he could of persons who had known the
mare four years. He did. Brought the mare back, and asked
for a warranty. I told him I should not give one, so he had
better keep his money; but he changed his mind, left the
money, and took the mare.

When the Duke returned from Jamaica there was not a
spaniel; and as he wished to have the clumber breed, I got
the first from Lord Jersey. After that we got some direct
from the Duke of Newcastle; then from Lord Middleton.
They are the best dogs for a long day and thick cover I know.
When nicely broke and down charge it is a noble sight to see
about four couple, with gentlemen, following the pheasants being first quietly driven into the young spring.
They are first-rate for woodcocks. I have frequently killed
five or six in a day, both at Swineshead and Honeyhill Woods;
and to see Col. T. M. Steele pull them and the cock-pheasants
de wnwas delightful. The only clumber spaniel that I know of,
now in this neighbourhood, is kept by James Wilson, Esq.
Pointers we were unfortunate with, as we never got into a
good breed.

G

When I first came to Kimbolton, forty-three years ago, it was a hard country for partridge shooting, and all the land needed draining, and there were no turnips or root crops grown. After the Duke had told me what he should like to do with the farm, he said, " There are two things I should like you to do as soon as you can, viz : to kill all the out-lying deer, as they do a great deal of mischief; and to set to work and kill down the rabbits, for the place is swarming with them." Other things we took as they came. He told me there was an old pensioner living at Staughton, a very quiet man, who would come with his dogs and go rabbiting with me any time I wanted him. In a short time I sent for the man whose name was Marshall. The first day we killed four or five dozen, and the next morning I sent them down to the castle, and told the woodmen to hang them up in the larder, and if they saw the Duke, and he enquired for me, to tell him I should be down in about ten minutes. When I got down, there the men stood with the rabbits on their poles against the castle. I asked them why they stood there. They said the Duke forbid having them taken into the castle, and wished to see me. I was to wait until he came up ; and in about ten minutes the Duke came, with the Duke of Gordon on his left arm ; and when within about twenty yards he called me to him and said' " Where did you kill all those rabbits ? " I said, " At the Warren Spinney, Your Grace." He said, " You have had a good day. How many ? " I said, " About four dozen, Your Grace." He said, " What are you going to do with them ? " I said, " I told the men to bring them here and hang them up in the larder, as I understand that is the custom of the place." He said, " I will do away with that custom." I said, " Your Grace wishes to have them killed, and if you will

say what I am to do with them, your orders shall be complied
with." He then caught hold of me by the arm, and led me
farther from the men, and said, " I will tell you what to do
with them : take and sell them, put the money in your
pocket, and take care of it; some day you will find it useful."
I thanked His Grace, and he turned to the Duke of Gordon,
saying, " Do you think Dale will like that?" The Duke of
Gordon smiled, and said, " I do not think he will object to
it." The Duke of Manchester then said, " Do it quietly;
let no one know they are your perquisites; if the farmers
get to know, they will be jealous, and you will soon have a
row. Neither tell the steward, as he would shoot and eat rabbits
all the year round; and never bring any to the castle, as I
would as leave eat a rat."

He turned to the Duke of Gordon, and said, " You will
go into the kitchen some day, and see that old woman
(meaning the housekeeper) smothered up in rabbits' fur, for
she is always after the skins." They were at that time worth
nine shillings per dozen. He then said to me, " My servants
are all on board wages, and I don't wish you to work for them.
You will require some nets : get what you want, and I will
pay for them, and all other expenses." I said, " If Your
Grace allows me the rabbits, I can pay the expenses." But
if I like to do it, you will not object ? " he asked. " Well,
no, my lord," I replied. He then told me that as he had
no dogs or ferrits I had better get old Marshall of Staughton,
as he was an old pensioner, and very quiet. After some talk
about other matters, he said, " Now go and send the men
back to your house with the rabbits, and we will soon be up
with you." I did so.

The Duke had now set me a job to kill and sell from fifteen

to twenty dozen rabbits a week, without people knowing.
The way I did was this : I took my nets in the night, run
them by the side of the wood, and then old Marshall run the
rabbits in with his dogs.   By moving our nets, and so having
various pitches during the night, we frequently caught several
dozens.   I sold them to old Marshall, and he took them away
on a small hand-truck, selling them to a man named Conry of
Eaton, who brought them back to Kimbolton, and sold them as
Sandy rabbits, Sandy lying some miles off.

    This went on for seven years.   The steward often asked me
what I did with the rabbits, but of course I always gave him
an evasive answer.   However, after seven years had rolled by
our dodge was discovered.   One night we had been out killing,
and as Marshall was going home with two sacks full, he was
overtaken by Neville Day, Esq., the lawyer, of St. Neots,
who had been dining with the steward, and was returning
home.   He asked him what he had got in his sacks, when
Marshall replied, " Dogs" meat, sir."   The lawyer said,
" That's a lie; I will see;" and springing from his horse,
opened the bags, and found they were rabbits.   " Where have
you brought them from?" he asked.   " If you want to know
more, you must go and ask Mr. Dale, as I am employed by
him."   He bought a couple, and took them home.   The next
morning he wrote to the steward and clergyman, to tell them
what he had discovered after leaving them the previous
night.   As soon as the Rev. J. T. H. had received the note,
which was brought by the lawyer's groom, he went direct to
the Duke, and told him the whole affair.   After the Duke
had listened to his story, he said, " Thank you, sir, for your
information ; but you are seven years behind-hand ; I give
Dale credit for keeping the Kimbolton people in the dark for

seven years." The parson then left with his head down, as it was not the first time he had talked to the Duke about me; but the Duke being a just and good man, always told me about the affair.

On the following Sunday, the steward sent for me. I went, and he told me all about it. He said he had dined with the Duke the night before, and wished me to know who it was that had informed the Duke. I thanked him, and told him that I had just left the Duke, and he had not said anything to me, and finding that I had dark looks from some of my old friends, and as some had even said that Ihadbeen a rogue, I should go back and ask the Duke whether he wished for a change or not.

As I entered the butler's pantry, the butler and gardener were talking it over. The gardener said he was sure I should lose my situation; to which the butler added : "Yes; and serve him right, a d——d rogue." On asking the butler as to where the Duke was, he told me I should find him in his room. The gardener was anxious to know what was the matter, but I told him that was my business, and went to the Duke. I told him what the steward had told me about the clergyman. "Ah," he said, "the fellow came to me the other day with a cockney boo story, fit to burst. I thanked him, and told him he was seven years behind; and I gave you credit for what you had done according to my orders." I then asked him if he wished any change. He said, "No; and if any one says anything to you about it, tell them to mind their own business, and not interfere with you; the parson as well; and tell them I told you to say so. Go on as you have been doing; I am quite satisfied."

At that time there were a great many rabbits at Shelton

Goss, and all the farmers were making great complaints The Rev. D. Crofts having the charge of the Goss covert, wished the rabbits to be killed without disturbing it. His nephew Mr. Thomas Bloodsworth said, "Uncle, will you allow me to ask Dale to bring his men and nets some night, and I will go with him and try to kill some quietly?" He answered, "You may go and try; but I know you cannot kill them that way.''

The nephew said, "Well, we will try." So he named it to me, and I fixed on a night, and drove over. Calling at the house, we were pressed upon to take something before we went, but Mr. Crofts said he felt sure we should do no good. I said, "Well, sir, we shall be back about eleven; you will not go to bed until we return?" Arriving there, we pitched our nets three times, and caught about six dozen. We then went back, and laid them on the kitchen floor, completely covering it, after which he went in to Mr. and Mrs. Crofts, and said, "Uncle, we have caught two or three; will you have them, or shall Mr. Dale have them for his trouble?" He said, "He may have them; I was sure you would not do any good; but I will come and speak to Dale." Judge, then, his surprise, when he saw such a large number lying dead. He was much pleased, and never forgotten to talk about it. I went several times after that, and he always gave me the rabbits for my trouble.

The first season I was with the Duke, and after the doe season, (we having killed about fifteen brace), he sent for me one morning into his room. After other business had been talked over, he asked how the steward and I went on as regarded the perquisites of the deer. I said, "I do not know, my lord.'' He said, "I do not intend for him to interfere: there is a knife and fork at my table when he likes to come; but I will not allow him to interfere either with the deer, the home farm, or shooting in the woods. I hope if he attempts when I am away, you will stop him. Go and tell him thah I wish you to take the charge, and no oue to interfere. I expect you to take the skins horns, fat and cuttings; if you like to give him a few of the shoulders, so well and good; I give him haunches and sides when he has company. Go, and hear what he says, and then let me know." I went and told him what the Duke wished me say, when he replied, " I shall not give them up, as they are all I get for my trouble." I said, " Sir, you will have no trouble, as the business is to be carried on by the Duke and myself." " Well," he said again, " I will not give them up." I said, " Very well, sir; then I am to take that message to the Duke, as he is waiting my return ? " " Well, tell the Duke I will see him," he said. So I went back to the Duke, and told His Grace that the steward woud see him, and that he did not at all like giving them up, The Duke, however, said, " He shall; you have possession, and you keep them. He has had everything since I have been away; I shall make a change now, for he has got plenty," When the man came to buy the skins, he was sent to me; so we got on with clouds; but as the Duke was at home ten months out of twelve, he kept us square; for he was a fine and good man, and few men knew better, or had seen more than the Duke of Manchester.

The buck season came on, and he wanted a buck. I told him there was oue lying in the fields of the farm near to Honey-Hill Wood; and he said if I would have my men ready, he would be at my house, and help me to kill him. We went and tried all over, but could not find him. So the Duke said, " Squire Fletcher will be here to-night; come down about six o'clock, and see him; perhaps he would like to go out with you in the morning with the blood-hounds, and have a shot at him."

I went down, saw Mr. Fletcher, and told him my mission, but he declined, on account of being tired, and wished me to kill it myself if I could.

I went to the Duke, and found him dressing for dinner, and informed him what Mr. Fletcher had said. He told me I might kill him if I could, but he doubted whether I should find me. I left the Duke as the clock struck seven, to go home to fetch my rifle; and seeing the groom, asked him to go with him. When we had got about half-a-mile from my house, I saw the buck feeding in the middle of a field of barley. I left the groom, telling him to stand quiet whilst I went a quarter of a mile, where he would make for. When I got to the place, the groom showed himself to the buck, and away he came; but just as he sprung to leap the hedge, I shot and killed him dead. The groom came up. After tying his legs together, we got a rail bar, slung him between us, and carried him home. I dressed him, and then returned to the castle, arriving there at nine o'clock exactly. I told the footman to tell the Duke that I had killed the buck. He did; but the Duke told him he was dreaming, and sent for me to go into the room. When I got there, he said, " Well, Dale, what about the buck ?" I said, " I have killed him, Your Grace." " Why did you not stop and dress him ?" he asked. I told him I had done all that, when he replied, "Quick work, too; why you have been only two hours; very quick." The clergyman was taking wine with the Duke and Mr. F., so the Duke said, " Take a glass of wine, Dale ?" I thanked His Grace. He then asked if I had cut him down, when I told him I had not, but would do so the first thing in the morning. He now rung the bell for the footman, and told him to set supper and ale for me and the groom, telling me as I left the room that he intended being up

early in the morning. I was up the next morning at three
o'clock and had just parted the buck, and about four, who
should come up but the parson; he knowing the Duke would
be early to look at the buck, but as the Duke was not there
he waited about until he came. Meantime, he said to me,
" Ah, he ought to have been parted last night. He will soon
spoil." About six the Duke came, and said, " Well, Mr.
Parson, where have you been?" The parson said, " The buck
is spoilt." " What the devil do you know about it? You
would have been better in bed," said the Duke. The parson
then went away. The Duke looked at the buck and said he
was a fine one, and well killed. I then went round the farm,
and he home to breakfast.

Just before this I told the Duke I wished to get married
if I remained with him. He said, " With all my heart, and
I am sure you will be more comfortable : do so, as soon as you
like. As I fell in love with Miss Sapcote, and she with me,
when we were only sixteen years of age, and had courted
seven years, I thought it would be nothing unreasonable, and
the Duke thought so too; so I accordingly got married.
But as the Duke wanted to know the full particulars, I must
inform my readers that my wife was the Grand-daughter of
my old school-mistress—Nanny Frisby; and a kinder wife and
mother never breathed, and was highly respected by all who
knew her.

One day the Duke was near being shot by Squire Fletcher.
I knew there was a fat buck lying in the long shrubbery, as
at that time the deer did not go down into the pleasure ground,
so I sent some men to turn him out. The Duke and I were
against a beech tree in the pleasure ground, and Squire
Fletcher under a thorn tree a little distance from us. The buck

H

was a fine one, and came between the castle and the place where we stood. I up'd with my rifle, but the Duke said, "Let Fletcher take the shot." He did: pointed across, but not at us, shot, missed the buck, and one of the balls struck a tree that was close to us and just the height of the Duke's head. So the buck went away untouched; and the Duke said he was sorry we did not shoot at him. When Fletcher came up, the Duke said, "What did you shoot at?" He said, "The buck." The Duke said, "Not a bit of it; you shot at us." He said, "I pointed at the buck." The Duke then showed him where the ball struck the tree, and there was no mistake as we heard it; and the scar can be seen in the tree to this day, although it is thirty-nine years ago. Had the Duke chosen that tree he would have been a dead man. The reason was—Mr. Fletcher had put two balls in his gun, and at a certain distance they touched each other; one flew one way, and the other the contrary; neither of them going straight to the buck. Two balls never ought to be put in at the same time.

After I had been some time with William, the fifth Duke of Manchester, he proposed that the bucks and does should be allowed to graze in the pleasure ground and round the castle. A new fence was ordered to be put down on the out-side at once, and as the Duke was going (in about ten days from the time the fence was ordered) to visit the late Duke in Ireland, and from there to the late Duke of Gordon in Scotland, he told me to see to it. He wanting to see the deer down in the pleasure ground before he went, the fence was put down temporary, and the day before he went, His Grace, myself, and all the men I had to spare tried to drive them down, but could not as the wind was against us, so we were obliged to give it up.

The next morning I was standing counting how many there were that had gone down during the night, when I saw the Duke come down the White Hall steps, with nothing more on than his slippers, night cap, and dressing gown. He walked along the terrace, and as it was about half-past two in the morning he could not see the deer for the fog that rose from the piece of water in front of the castle which was between him and them. After he had walked backwards and forwards for about half-an-hour he returned up the steps into the castle, and I saw no more of him until he sent for me at nine o'clock, when he was at breakfast with Squire Fletcher. He said he was sorry they would not come down. I told him a few had been down during the night. He said, " Not a bit of it." I said, " Yes, my lord; there were twenty-eight in when Your Grace came down the steps at half-past two." He said, " Where were you?" I said, " upon the hill in the park under the large wytch tree," which caused him to laugh and say, " All right." That day he started on his journey very cheerfully.

One night just before he went away we were passing the house of one of our old carpenters, whose name was Grant. He was sixty years of age, and very fond of ale. Sometimes on a Saturday night he had but very little money left when the ale he had drank during the week was paid for. He had a daughter about forty years of age, who was living at home with her mother. The week before, he went home drunk, and as his wife and daughter were putting him to bed, he heard the mother say to the daughter, " If he comes home like this any more we will give him a good thrashing." The day we were passing he came home staggering, but only professing to be drunk. When they had put him to bed, the mother

H2

said to the daughter, " Now, Soph, hold that arm, and I will
hold this ; and I will pummel him well, now." At that
moment he was lying on his back with his arms across his
breast, when he struck them out, hiting both in the face,
which made the blood fly. They came crying down and told
us the whole affair. The Duke gave them something, and
the next day old Grant was severely reproved by him, which
I say he deserved. William, the fifth Duke of Manchester
was very kind to all who tried to do their duty. I have guns
and other things by me now, which were given to me as pres-
ents from His Grace, as well as several other things from
other branches of the family. The best double barrel
gun I ever shot with, was made for me by Mr. J. Bull, High
Street, Bedford. He also made a beautiful double barrel rifle
for a friend of mine that would kill at a very long distance.
At that time Mr. J. Bull and I were very good friends, and
I always found he did his best to please his customers.

But to return to old Grant. The Duke was keeping him
out of charity, as he was not only getting old, but his frame
was very much shattered by execessive drinking.

Now let me beg of my readers, both old and young, to
abstain from to much of all intoxicating drinks, and to shun
gambling and all kinds of betting ; otherwise, like me, they
may have cause to repent, as I once did in my early courting
days. I was about twenty years of age, and was living with
the Right Hon. Lady Willoughby de Ersby. I drove my
intended wife and her sister to Stamford races, and pulled up
opposite the grand stand. When the first race was over,
their brother came up on horseback, and at the time about
twelve men collected together, and I could see that some sort
of a game was going on between the races, so I said to my

young ladies' brother, " George, will you hold my horse for a few minutes, I shall soon be back ?   He said, " Yes, I will." I was soon over the ropes and among the strangers.   Some of them were dressed as gentlemen's servants, some as farmers, others as tradesmen of different kinds, and some as gentle-men, all of which (as I was told afterwards) belonged to the same firm.   They had all been playing amongst themselves, but as I was the first fool to be caught, as soon as I had made my appearance at the table and had got as close to the thimbles and peas as I could, (there being a pile of half-crowns, Crowns, and soverings as a draw,) my left-hand man began to bet on the pea, and I took great interest in the game, and thought the movement of the man with the thimble very simple, and the man that was playing kept loosing and winning alter-nately, but thinking I could see where he was wrong, I put down my half-crown, and bet that I could name the thimble the pea was under.   I named a thimble, and it was lifted up, but the pea was not under ; and so on, until I had lost ten shillings almost as quickly as I could tell it, which I was ashamed to do for years after.   I then went back into the gig to my company, but was silent about my speck of luck : it was the first and last of my gambling.   I have since seen men loose all the money they had with them at *that* and similar games.   I have tried to prevent them, but my advice was not heeded until too late.

I am grieved to say how many families I have seen destitute of necessary comforts through drink ; others, with the same number of children, have been in the possession of every comfort, through being steady, frugal, and industrious.

I am afraid the new system of Education will prove injurious both to the labourer and tenant farmer.   The parents will miss the money which some of their children had been in the habit of earning; while the farmers will greatly miss their services upon the land and about the yard for different purposes. If the children were nicely taught and cared for up to eight years old, and then sent to a good night school from eight to fifteen or sixteen, they might be brought out scholars good enough for anything that might be required of them. I have been told that it would be too much for the boys to go to school after a day's work; but to that I answer, No! It would be much better for them; and much more respectable than playing all sorts of mischief that is generally practised by them where there is not any night school. I know it by experience, and could enlarge greatly upon this and other subjects, which might not occupy the time of my readers to any good purpose, as I believe in the old proverb, "Great talkers and great writers are little doers." So I will drop the subject, hoping I have said enough to set others thinking.

CHAPTER V.

The father of the late Lord Willoughby was very kind and good to all; and his delight was to see the poor made comfortable. After the death of his mother—the Right Hon. Lady Willoughby, he came in possession of the Grimsthorpe estate, and several adjoining parishes, and Little Bytham was one of them. On his first ride round that village he saw two very old cottages in a dilapidated state; especially the one occupied by Polly Clapton, (as she was called,) which was also very filthy. His Lordship gave orders to the steward that they should be pulled down and rebuilt as quickly as possible, so that they should be comfortable. The steward gave orders to the bailiff who was to see that they were done, as he lived in London, and was only at Little Bytham twice a year.

The first opportunity his Lordship had after the cottages were finished, he took the steward and bailiff to look at them. They viewed them up-stairs and down, and looked in all the closets and out-houses, and thought they would do. His Lordship turned to Polly with the steward on one side and the bailiff on the other, and said, " Well, now, Polly, I hope you will keep clean ; and I think you have got all you want, now."

She was then as she mostly was—dotted all over with flea dirts, and said, " Oh, no; that I have not. We hav'nt a pigstye: they would not build us one." His Lordship said, " Oh, dear; what not a pigstye? You shall have one." Polly said, " Yes, you say so. But there's that old Kennedy; he wont let it be done when you are gone away, I know." She not knowing it was Mr. Kennedy at his Lordship's right hand, his Lordship smiled and said, " Oh, yes; I will speak to Mr. Kennedy. I think he will let you have it. Good day." And off they went much amused.

My way of choosing and buying a horse, was to go to Bowden or some other fair, where there were large droves of Welsh or Irish ponies. As you cannot get amongst them to choose for being kept so closely together by the dealer and his men, and as I was short on the leg, I used to get upon a gate, style, waggon, cart, or something of the sort to enable me to look over them. If I could see a good head and neck about three years old, I gave orders to have him brought out; and I was always fortunate enough to happen of a good one, for there is generally something useful behind a good head and neck. After I had made a bargain, I would take him home and rest him awhile; then set to and break and train him; but I never on any account used a stick or whip to hit him with. I punished with spurs if required, but not otherwise. Nither do I like punishing severely as some people do. It is best to keep your horse's temper as quiet as possible, and treat him with kindness. I have heard many people say their horse would use his left leg first. The cause is—they use their stick with the right hand, and the spur on the right leg, which causes him to cringe and throw out his left leg first. Punish him gently on the near side, and draw the bit by the near rein, and he will bring his right leg out first. Carry a few oats in your pocket, and give him a few occasionally when you are leading him, and he will soon follow or come to you when you hold up your hand. I have had some very good ones, as the people in Kimbolton know. The spur I used to wear for every day use, was a spur with the neck cut off and a rowel put in close to the plate, which I used to wear on my left foot.

Horses and dogs are very sagacious. We know that it is better to please than to tease a fool; and if such treatment is the best with man, so it is with dumb animals. Certainly, circumstances alter cases; but a little punishment properly administered does good, as with children.

William, the fifth Duke of Manchester, used to say, "If you see a man that neither a child nor dog will notice, that man is not worth much.

The only time I was near getting into trouble through a girl, was at Nottingham, in the year 1826, which was before I was married. Three of my young male friends and I had crossed the Market Place and going along a street, when at the North-east corner, the same number of girls came up behind and put their arms around us, and asked if we would go their way, to which my friends agreed, and walked on together. But as I refused to go, I had to free myself from her grasp; which I did, by shoving her up against a door. The door opened, and she fell backwards down three or four steps into the house; and a dog that was inside seized her, which caused her to cry out murder. I stepped over to the other side of the street, and stood there quietly until the row was over. I then went home to my relations, escaped all right. It was then eleven o'clock at night.

I

On one occasion the Duke sent for me and said he should
like to have a buck killed as soon as possible, but not liking
to drive them as the weather was very hot, he said he would
go with me and have a shot himself, as we did occasionally.
He was a very good shot with a rifle, and we often practised
together.   As we did not succeed in killing the buck that day
we went home, and I asked the Duke if I should kill one if
they came round.   He said, " No, let it be until to morrow."
I said, " To-morrow is Sunday."   He said, " Never mind
about that."   So on Sunday about two o'clock he came riding
up with his groom behind.   My wife and I were at dinner.
He said, " Dale, we must have a buck."   I said, " Very well,
Your Grace."   He said, " But how is he to be had?   They
are lying in a place where they cannot be got at; but should
they come near, kill one if you can.   I am now going to see
General Honslow, and shall be back in about an hour, and if
you have not killed one by that time, I will help you to get
one."   So I told my wife to put away the things whilst I
loaded my rifle, which, as soon as she had done, she took my
arm, and we walked down to the deer. They laid under a clump
of trees as the day was very hot.   My wife and I were dressed
in black, as she had lately buried her only sister.   We put
them up and moved them about so as to get a fine buck out
clear, and as soon as I had a good chance I shot at him and
knocked him down.   A man happened to be coming down the
public path at the time whom I sent to the house for a scratch,
which, as soon as he had fetched, we took him home and
dressed him, and when all was done, I went into the house
and sat down as before.   When the Duke came back and had
changed his horse and coat, he said, " Come, Dale, we must
have a buck!"   I said, " I have killed one, my lord."   He

said, " Why have you not dressed him then?" I said, " I
have done all." The Duke then went to look at him and was
very pleased, and said he never knew one killed and dressed so
quickly before. The deer went back and laid under the same
trees again. The Duke laughed when I told him I went in
my black coat and took my wife on my arm, and did not forget to talk about it afterwards. Had I gone alone I should
not have got near them; but as it was, they were deceived:

The venison was wanted for an election dinner at Huntingdon; and that is why the buck was killed on a Sunday. I
think the day he was cooked was the last time the late Duke
was returned for the county, and a good lark we had. The
day before, Mr. George of Bythorn, who was one of the Duke's
party, was in the Market Place, Huntingdon, where he was
grossly insulted by the " blue party," who set upon him, tore
his coat, knocked his hat over his eyes, and drove him down
into the George-yard. He then hired of Mr. Hennessey, the
landlord, the top room in the George Hotel that faced the gate-
way, unknown to anyone. He then took his horse and went
off home; but before he went to his own house, he went and
picked sixteen of the best men out of Bythorn and neighbourhood, collected them together, put them into a waggon, and
sent them off to Huntingdon to be put into the top room of the
George Hotel, where they arrived at three o'clock in the morning. They were only to have one pint of beer each and a
small quantity of food before they were called out. They were
all dressed in short slops and low-crown hats with a mark
round each so that they should know each other. Dinner was
ordered at three o'clock in the afternoon for a large party. Mr.
George was there, but he had not shown himself in the town.
The " blue party" from St. Ives were looking out for him,

but as they could not find him, they said he dare not show himself; but when dinner was over, and before the cloth was cleared, he left the table and walked up to the Town Hall, when, as soon as the roughs saw him, they set upon him and followed him down into the George-yard, when he cried out, " Now, my men ; out of the room." His men came down as quickly as possible, when he said to them, " Now my boys ; go at them ! Give it to them !" They did, and drove them over the bridge ; and I think some of them got a ducking in the river. After that Mr. George's excitement was over, and he enjoyed himself.

He was a good friend to me. He gave me the offer of two farms : one at Guilesbury, and the other at Spratten, upon an estate he was steward over ; but I did not accept of them, as he was about to give up the stewardship, being then far advanced in years. The land was very much out of order, and the landlord refused to assist the in-coming tenant.

CHAPTER VI.

As I have said in a previous chapter, the deer were very small. The park being very wet, it made it bad lying-out for them in the winter. The Duke said he would have the park and farm well drained; but as our men did not understand the work, I sent for some men whom I knew had been draining a great deal of land for Lord Howe, and also upon the estate of Lord Stamford. Sixteen of them came the first year; but after that, we did not have so many, as we worked our own men in with them by degrees, and in a few years they were able to do the work as well as them; and by so doing, we occupied our own men and kept the money in our own parish.

When we drained the " Back Sides," it was necessary to cut a deep drain to get the water to pass into the Pound Lane, and by doing so, we took away the supply from the town pump, which soon caused it to be dry: a thing which no one had witnessed before. I named it to the Duke, and he understood it at once; and had a drain turned into the town well, as well as into the Pound Lane.

At the same time, the fish-pond was made at the back of the warren; and soon after it was finished, and full of water, I was near losing my life.   It was one very hot summer's day, when Gordon, who was the gardener, proposed that I, Jacklin the keeper, the groom, footman, and himself should go and have a bathe in the new fish-pond.   I being no swimmer, it was arranged that the groom and footman, who were good swimmers, should teach me.   Unknown to me and the groom, Gordon proposed to the footman, that when we got about halfway across, where it would be about nine feet of water, he should give me a ducking; which he did at the place named.   We went in, and the groom took me about halfway across, when I said to him, "Leave go; I think I can get across, now."   As soon as he had left go, the footman came and caught hold of me by the back of the head, and sent me to the bottom, head first.   By struggling I rose so as to see them, but went down again.   I heard the groom say, "You fool, Joe!   If we do not catch hold of him next time he will be drowned."   Gordon was still sitting on the bank with his clothes on, and I heard him say, "No.   He wont hurt for ten minutes."   The groom said, "If we don't catch him the next time he rises we shall loose him."   When I rose the second time, one of them caught me by the hair of my head and dragged me out.   If I had not been exhausted, and for the water that had gone down my throat, I would have paid the footman and Mr. G. for their trouble.   I felt all that when I was under the water.   At that time the water was very muddy.

The next winter, we had a rare laugh at the poor groom.   I was going to take bucks, when the groom came up to me in the park on a cob we had bought of the late Lord Middleton.   It was a good pony for shooting.   John said, "I am sure I could

get a buck out of that herd with this pony." I was sure he
could not gallop more than seven miles in an hour, and refused
to let him try ; but Col. Steele said, "Let him try, and that will
satisfy him. His pony will not gallop far; and it will take a
little of the 'know' out of John." I showed him the buck I
wanted ; and away John went. He had not been at it long,
when in jumping a small ditch, the girt broke, and John and
saddle both slipped off behind on to the ground. The buck ran
away, and the pony went home at a gentle trot, quite tired of
galloping. John took up his saddle and off he went, which
caused a good laugh amongst the ladies and gentlemen.

The next spring, Lord Mandeville (now Duke of Manchester) and I got into trouble. He was in London, and wrote to
me to know if there were any fawns to shoot. I wrote back and
said there were, and fixed on a day for him to come down. He
came; and his father sent for me as they were taking their wine in
the drawing room. The Duke said, "Well, Dale; Mandy is come."
I said, "I am glad to see his Lordship well." He said, "Now
make your own arrangements." I said, "I should like to be at
it by four o'clock in the morning." Then said the Duke, "You will
have to go by yourself, for you will never get Mandy so early."
Mandy said, "Yes, you will, Dale; if you come and call me."
I was up the next morning at half-past three, and went and threw
some shot at Lord Mandeville's window, when he was soon up,
dressed, and out. We were quickly at our work ; and by eight
oclock, we had killed fourteen. I said, "Now, my lord; if you
will go home, you will surprise the Duke ! And when you have
had a rest, bring up your rifle ; and we will have a few shots with
the ball." He had scarcely got a hundred yards from me, when
my son came to me on my horse, and said, "Father ; the deer
are all getting through the fence and going across the fields !"

I then galloped to them, and placed myself between them and the fence, and shot both barrels off, but I could not stop them. They galloped for two miles, when I headed and succeeded in turning them; and within a fortnight, I had all back in the park but four, and they were not out a month. We did not loose a single deer, although we had several enemies at work, who tried all they could to get some of them; but we will say no more about that.

I must add, that the steward had persuaded the Duke to have a seven-wire fence put down round the outside, which a drove of donkeys might creep through with ease.

The last buck that remained out was caught by my dog, Sailor, in a field on the Home Farm. I had to lead him some distance to the park, and when I got him inside I let him go. He went about ten yards, then turned round and came at me with great force. I caught him by one of his horns, and doubled my whip-thong and stock together, and gave him five or six strokes across the ribs, then let him go. He never came at me any more after that. He was a seven-year old buck, and as it was in September, he was very strong, and I was not very weak at that time.

About that time, I carried Dale, the coachman, who weighed seventeen stone, and ran fifty yards with him; while the footman ran one hundred. I won by five yards. They were living with Col. Steele, but were then staying at the castle.

I am glad to inform my readers that the then Lord Mandeville is now Duke of Manchester; and has had some first-rate new wire fences put down; so that there is no fear of any deer getting out of the park through them.

One year, my son and I killed thirteen dozen wood-pigeons in six weeks. The farmers complained that they injured their crops, which I knew they did. They sometimes complained about the rooks without any just cause. I have proved that the good they do exceeds the evil. A pigeon will take sixty peas per day.

At that time we had a good rookery; and the Duke liked to see a few about the farm; although we usually killed from seventy to eighty dozen a year. The Duke always allowed me to give the trades-people who were fond of a gun a half-day's shooting, which they enjoyed very much, whether he was at the castle or not.

A gentleman from Scotland was once on a visit to the late Duke of Manchester, and as we were walking over the Park Farm, he told us that his tenants, some few years before, had complained about him keeping too many rooks, and petitioned him to do away with his rookery, which he very reluctantly did to pacify them after a long " parley," in which they thought they were right. But after three years, they came and said they had found out they were wrong, as they could not grow such good crops as before, in consequence of the increase of the wireworm.

On one occasion I was with the Duke in his room, and he said, " When are you going to shoot the rooks?" I said, " When you please, my lord." He said, " Well, say to day. Who do you ask?" I told him. He said, " All right. Perhaps I may bring my gun and have a few shots, but do not wait for me." I went down to the pantry and asked the butler if he would join us. He wanted to know who was going; and when I had told him, he said, " What, that lot of scamps! If they go, I wont join you." I must say that B. Welstead, Esq., was to be amongst us. I told him if he liked to come I would bring him a gun and find him what powder and shot he required; but he said he

J

would not come near.   When that man came after his situation at the Duke's, he had to borrow a suit of clothes to appear respectable in.

A few days afterwards, several of us were fishing, the Duke also; and I shall never forget the event of the day.   The Duke was on one side of the water and wanted a rope that was on ours, so he asked Jacklin the keeper to throw it to him.   He tried, but could not.   others tried; Robinson the woodman tried; but neither succeeded in getting it across.   The Duke then called for me to throw it.   I did, the wind caught it, and it fell on the Duke and wrapped tight round his neck.   He held his head down and shook it off, and said, " D—— it!   Are you going to hang me ?"   I apologized, but he said, " Never mind, as long as it is over; I know you did not do it for the purpose."

The next day, he told me to take two of the under gardeners and the keeper to the castle, and see that they had some ale; for he knew some that he sent had to go away with small-beer, and some without any.   The Duke walked down to the castle, and said again as he went to dress, " See that they have some ale."   I said, " Thank you, my lord; I will."   I looked for the butler, and found him; he looked as black as the rooks, which showed to me that he had not forgotten them.   I asked him for some ale for the men; and he asking how many, I told him four.   He took the copper, went into the small-beer cellar, and set the tap running, which I could hear; and did not go to the ale cellar at all.   He brought it to me, and I gave it to the keeper first, after I had tasted it myself, but did not say anything.   I then gave some to Maile for him to taste, and thought as he had some small-beer every day he would be the best judge.   As soon as Maile had tasted he

said, " I am sure it is small-beer." I said, " I am sure so
too." I told him to keep the copper until I could see the
butler. Presently he came for the pudding, as the Duke was
dining alone, when I told him he had given me small-beer.
He said it was ale, and went on. I followed him into the
kitchen and said, " Do you mean to give me ale for those
men or not ?" He said, " You have got ale." I said, " No; it
is small-beer." He said, " You are a liar." I said, " It is
you that is the liar." He put his napkin under his arm,
came up with his fists clenched, and said, " If you say I am a
liar again, I will knock you down." I met him and said, " If
you dare to do it I will spoil your face before you take up the
Duke's pudding. I should like five minutes at you." He
turned round and went off with the pudding, then I followed
him to the dining-room door, and would have went in with
the beer in my hand, had he not have begged of me to go
back and said he would draw me some ale, which he did soon
after, but never spoke.

The next morning, Mrs. Daniels said to me, " What a ter-
rible little man you are, Dale ; I wish you had given him a
good thrashing, for I am sure he deserved it." She told me
she had been housekeeper and cook in that castle for nearly
fifty years, and she never was treated so badly by anyone as she
was by the butler. She was sure the Duke did not know,
but she hoped I would tell him, as she and the kitchen maid
were witnesses as well as the men. I told her I would not
that time, as he had a wife and family to keep; but if he
served me so again I would. She said, " If you don't tell him
I will." Afterwards, the Duke heard something had been
wrong, and asked her what it was ; and she told him all that
passed. The next week the Duke took him to London, but

did not bring him back again ; and I heard afterwards that he came to poverty.

Mr. L. J. Ibbs was very fond of the gun, and a walk at that time pleased him much. We were once invited out to a day's shooting at Great Gidding, in the month of October. It was agreed that I should take breakfast at his house at four o'clock in the morning, in order that we might get out of Kimbolton before the people began to stir. When we had got about half-a-mile from the town, it was sufficiently light for us to see a partridge. We started our pointer, and beat the fields, until we came to our friend's house at Gidding. Arriving there at eleven o'clock, we found about twelve gentlemen from Peterborough and other places, amongst whom was Lord Fitzwilliam's keeper. They were taking lunch ; and as several hours had expired since we breakfasted, we were quite ready and very glad to join them. Dinner was ordered for three. As it was proposed that we should walk the fields abreast, directly we started and had got into a line, I saw that several of our party, which composed about fourteen, did not know how to carry a gun so as to be perfectly safe, for both on my right and left I could see down the barrel of their guns, and I thought possibly some one might get shot. I noticed that my friend Mr. Ibbs was looking at the same thing, his countenance becoming serious. I went and spoke to him, as I found he kept a little behind the front rank. He said, " This wont do ; there will be an accident." So I went and spoke to the keeper, and asked whether he would allow Mr. Ibbs and myself to walk together. He said he had no objection, and suggested that we should work to the left and they would go to the right. I then went back for my pointer, which I had shut up, thinking it would be unsafe with the whole party. I remarked to Mr. Ibbs that I thought we should beat the lot, an observation which proved very true. Returning at three o'clock, we found we were last; and on entering the kitchen, saw the game laid out which they had killed. They had washed, and gone into the room for dinner; so I asked the servant whether that was all the game they brought home, and on her replying in the affirmative we took ours out, which made a much larger display than all theirs.

Having washed, we followed into the dining-room, and told our worthy host what we had done. It amused him much, as he was not one of the party, being no shot. We had a splendid dinner; and after taking our wine, and tea being talked about, I asked my friend if he felt inclined to walk and shoot our way back, a proposal to which he agreed with all his heart.

When we reached Spaldwick, it was quite dusk; so we walked into an inn kept by a Mr. Martin, a sporting gent. Over our glass and pipe, (which we much enjoyed) he told us what a capital day's shooting he and his friends had had at Kimbolton, over Mr. Mason's farm, adjoining the Duke's, where they had trespassed and found first-rate shooting, and as they did not meet with Jacklin the keeper, they should try it again, and give the Duke another benefit. Not knowing me, and knowing Mr. Ibbs to be a man not to interfere with other people's business, they did come; but as I had given the keeper orders to be on the look out for them, he happened to catch them, which spoilt their sport. We arrived at Kimbolton by nine o'clock, and Mrs. Ibbs got us a good tea, with ham and everything first-rate; and as Dr. Verrity once said, I thought Mr. Ibbs was a happy man, with one of the best wives in Kimbolton. We afterwards had a smoke, and parted about eleven o'clock. We had walked about forty miles, and both felt and said we could go the same over again without rest, and I believe we could have done so.

While out rook-shooting, the Duke shot one near to the castle, so that it lodged on the top of a large tree in the ice-house yard, the groom contending with the Duke with a deal of " Yes, Your Grace," and " No, Your Grace," which he was not very fond of, the Duke said, " Yes, Your Grace, and No, Your Grace, and d—— Your Grace, come straight to the point." To prove the Duke was right, I set to and climbed the tree, which was very high, brought down the rook, and left my watch hanging at the top, the ring having caught the rough bark of the tree and pulled it out of my pocket. I did not miss it until the next morning, as we had spent the evening at the castle, and did not get home until late. I looked for it in every place I could think of, and made all inquiries, but could neither see nor hear anything of it. Next morning, I thought of the tree, and on going to look, saw it hung at the top; so I had to climb a second time the tree which the groom said could not be climbed by any one.

The Duke was always fond of a joke. One day we were going to shoot in Honey Hill Wood; the Duke of Gordon, General Honslow, Squire Fletcher, and the Duke of Bedford accompanying us. The Duke was singing and whistling on his pony, a little ahead of the rest. All at once he said, " Dale, what dogs have they got to-day?" I told him their names. He said, " Will they be hunting in Swineshead wood at the same time we are shooting in Honey Hill Wood?" I said, " No, my lord." [The woods were a mile apart.] He said, " Very good," and went on as usual. He was always very cheerful on these occasions, and when at the wood sometimes he would say, "There are no pheasants." At other times, and very soon after, "Ah! it's no use shooting; you may as well shoot amongst a flock of dove-house pigeons." He knew our dogs could not be beaten for good behaviour, and every one felt delighted to see them do their work.

The Duke always expressed himself as well satisfied during the fifteen years I lived with him. He was always very kind to me and my family, and indeed to every one about him, if they did but do their duty; but if they neglected that, they were soon sent off. He was never better pleased than when he could get Mr. George of Bythorn, Mr. Ladds of Ellington, Mr. Fairy of Covington, or Mr. Horsford of Stow, over, to talk and look over the Home Farm, which he was very fond of, and on which he spent the most of his time during the first ten years I was with him.

As we were once riding through the Park we witnessed an affair which very much amused us. I had put a young man on to spud thistles, who had an idea that he should like to be a soldier. Not noticing us, he pulled off his coat, stuck his spud down, squared at it, and knocked it down; and continued these operations until we rode up to him. His name was John Hornsey, and he told us why he was practising. I believe he enlisted, but what became of him afterwards I do not know.

Another man, called Jimmy Dean, formerly post boy at the Lion inn, who, when he got old no one would employ; so the Duke wished me to put him to a light job. We went to him one day, when the Duke said, " Jimmy, how often do you clean your teeth?" " Once a year, Your Grace." " When's that, Jimmy?" the Duke asked. "At our club feast, Your Grace; I get plenty of beef on that day, and I find that cleans my teeth better than anything else," The Duke said, " Call at

the Castle as you go home, and I will order you something
to clean them with, and Dale will see that you have it." He
thanked His Grace, and we rode off. Coming to the back side
which was then fenced from the Park, there had been two
beautiful Devon beast feeding for some time, being almost too
much grass. As I had told him before, they were lying down
with their heads close to the ground to keep the flies off, as
at that time it was very hot. We could not see them, and he
thought they had got out. I said, "No, my lord, we shall
see them soon," repeating at the same time there was too
much grass. "Not a bit of it," he said, "there is not enough
for a jack rabbit.

One day we were trying to kill a buck, and as the Duke
was about to shoot, a woman was coming along the foot-path,
who cried out, "Pray don't shoot, sir; I'm in the family-
way." The Duke laughed and waited until she was gone.
The following season, it happened that the same woman was
crossing the park when the same thing occurred. The Duke
waiting until she passed, when she said, "You may shoot now,
sir; I am not in the family-way."

I found it the same here as at Grimsthorpe. If there was
any poaching going on I was called in. It happened about
three o'clock one morning, when my men heard somebody
shoot off twice in Honey Hill Wood, that they came and called
me up, told me what they had heard, and said they could not
come up with them. I got up and went to the wood, and as
it had been a little snow during the night, I soon hit upon
their track, and traced them down to some gipsies' tents. I
went quietly, looked in, and saw two men singeing hedgehogs
which their dogs had found. After they had singed them
and took out their inside, they would keep until they were

them. They had roasted one, the fat of which looked nice and rich. They said it was very good, and invited me to taste. I begged to be excused, and told them I suspected them of being in the wood, and if they were not off before nine o'clock I should bring the constable and move them; but before that time they were all gone.

A few nights afterwards, about ten o'clock, and very dark, as I was riding home sharp from Bedford, a man sprung at my horse and tried to hold him. He said, "Wo." But I was as quick as he, and said, "Oh, no." At the same time, putting my spurs to my horse, which was a very good one, and striking the man across the arm with a good stick I had in my hand, and by so doing I passed on, and neither saw nor heard anything more of him.

One day I was going down to the castle by the piece of water called the bason, when up flew seven wild ducks, a thing I had not seen before at Kimbolton; the waters being very much exposed, wild ducks would not stop, so we used to kill all we could. Colonel Steele had just before sent up to say he was going with Lady Elizabeth and family to spend a few days with Lady Olivia Sparrow, and wished to see me. The ducks rose from the middle of the pond, and at that time high reeds grew all round it, they flew round, and as I passed on at a quick pace, they soon settled again in the middle. Meeting Colonel Steele, I told him what I had seen, and asked whether he felt inclined to bring his gun and to lend me one, remarking that we might as well have some of them as not. However, he did not care to act upon my suggestion, but said he would walk to the pond with me and see them. When we reached it they started up and flew by us within gun shot. He was then vexed because we were without our guns.

K

I turned away, not thinking to see them again. About two o'clock as I was going towards the park pond I saw them again. I went back as quickly as possible, and fetched my double-barrel as well as my large bored single gun, and went round so as not to be seen until I came under the side of the pond. With double-barrel in hand, I stood up ; they rose in an instant. I knocked down two with the first shot, and two more with the second ; then taking up my single-barrel, down came another, at about sixty yards. Two gentlemen who were at a short distance, seeing what was going on, came running towards me, otherwise I should have killed the lot, as some were only winged, and were fluttering in the water. I should have secreted myself in a bed of rushes, and re-loaded ; they would sure to have settled down to the wounded birds, and I have no doubt I should have killed the whole of them.

I sent to Colonel Steele to say what I had done, and if he wished I would send them to him. His answer was: " Tell Dale we have plenty of good things at Brampton, so he had better eat them in his own family. The Duke was abroad, or I should have sent them to him, as he was very fond of anything of that kind.

About 1843 our good old Duke died abroad. Six months afterwards, the late Duke came one day to the castle, and asked me how things were going on. He said, " I am making a change ; I shall not form an establishment here for five years, but shall be here occasionally ; and if you like to do for me as you have done for my father, I wish you to continue on, as I desire no change with you." I told him I should be glad to do so, and after further conversation he left for Brampton.

Everything went on well for five years ; the tenants were

pleased with the Duke as a landlord, and the servants liked him as a master. All showed it by meeting in the White Hall twice a year at the rent audit, when we used to enjoy ourselves very much. But however, at the expiration of the time above stated, the Duke had occasion to change his steward, and unfortunately met with a man who was no more fit for the office than I should be for a parson. He soon put all things out of order, and nothing good for the Duke. Unfortunately I gave offence at his first coming. The Duke wished me to make a change at the bottom of the park, in doing away with a piece of water called the kennel. It was a work of time, as I wished to carry the thing out according to the Duke's plan, which I told him I would if no one was allowed to interfere between him and myself. He said they should not; he would tell each steward, the one going and the other coming, which he did, and the latter in my presence. This caused the new steward to show his teeth, although he did not dare to bite until he had been in office nearly two years, having got all the "know" out of me that he could. The Duke wished me to give him all the information I could; and I did so, as I found he had very little of the right sort of "know" in him.

I lost in the Duchess a good friend. I had been amongst ladies for many years, but none had been so kind to me as she had. If anything was reported wrong, she would tell at once, and it was soon put straight if anything really was wrong; but it was so often that her and the Duke were misled by false reports.

Some time before her death she took my eldest daughter as maid to her only daughter—Lady Olivia Montague, now Countess of Tankerville. But after the death of the Duchess,

K2

the Duke told me that he wished to keep on the Duchess's maid for Lady Olivia, and that my daughter Jane must come home, until Lady Olivia Sparrow and other ladies he had spoken to, could find a situation to suit her.   I thanked him, and took it as very kind of him.   But in a few months my wife died, and I was left with nine children, all at home, the youngest about two years old, so that I was obliged to keep my daughter at home.

Before the change of stewards a thing occurred which displeased the Duke much.   He had been in Ireland for some months, when I received a letter from him to say he would be at the castle on such a day, which he was.   He was soon up at my house and the farm.   The wind being right to take the foul smell from the stack yard, he came to the house and said, what a smell of mice, he was sure we had some in the stacks.   I told him we had only a stack and a half left.   He went to look and saw the roof falling in, when he said, do set the men to thrash it out.   I told him the steward thought it would make more money for keeping. It was not my fault.   This was in March.   The next week it was thrashed.   Out of the stack and a half we killed eleven thousand five hundred mice, and ninety six rats.   Lord Fred Montague was with us all the time.   I scarcely need inform my readers that the wheat was worth but very little.

At the time Lord Mandeville, now Duke of Manchester, and Lord Robert Montague were at Cambridge, (at least during their holidays,) I received a letter from Lady Olivia Sparrow, to say they would like a day or two's hunting, if I would get their horses ready and accompany them through the day.   They hoped to arrive at ten o'clock on Saturday morning in her carriage, to hunt with the Oakley hounds; I and the horses were ready.   The meet was at Swineshead wood. We found a fox and away we went. Mr. Magniac, the master of the hounds came up to me when they were a distance off, and said, " What young gents have you with you to-day, Dale." I said, " Lord Mandeville and Lord Robert Montague." He said, " I wish you would introduce me to them ; I will give you an opportunity. ' I said, " I will, sir." They saw him talking to me and came up, and wished to know who he was. So we soon came together. We had a long day. They whipped off about three miles beyond Colworth House, quite dusk. As we came along Mr. Magniac overtook us, and said, " Now my Lords, you must put in at my house, and take lunch with me ; your horses shall have some gruel. Dale knows my butler well. And then you will all go home comfortable." The invitation was accepted. We came across the country when it was as dark as pitch, and got home about nine o'clock. As soon as Mr. and Mrs. Ainsworth knew they were all well at home, they set the bells ringing.

Our next day was with the Fitzwilliam hounds at Buckworth wood. They had a nice day, but Lord Robert rode before the hounds and got scolded by Seabright the huntsman. The horse to cool himself jumped into a brook, which rather took the shine off the new scarlet. Lord Mandeville rode well and came home alright.

After I had been twenty-two years in the service the new steward found he could swim by himself, and he would put the check on me. We had been settling our accounts one day in January, all was right. I took my hat to leave the room, when he said, " Dale, I shall take your perquisites off' at Lady-day." I said, " Not with me ; if that is what you mean, you may get a man in my place three months to Lady-day. I shall leave, because the Duke had told me I should have them as usual ; and had the Duke changed his mind he would have told me so himself."

I would have yielded, but not from a man that did nothing right himself.

I saw two horses dead in a fortnight, through eating whole beans. They were worth one hundred pounds. I told the Duke he would not please him two years, if he did not see he would feel it. Afterwards he told Mr. Ainsworth that he found what I said to be true.

CHAPTER VII.

I left at Lady-day, and took an inn at Castle Bytham with a little land attached, until I could meet with a farm to suit me, as Lord Willoughby had promised me anything that might be at liberty; as well as sir John Trollope, and the Marquis of Exeter.

After I had been at the Inn at Castle Bytham about one year and a half, the Earl of Harborough offered me one.

I had a rough job at Castle Bytham, as the place was full of navvies. They were making the Great Northern Railway at that time. They were a rough lot, but I found some of the natives quite as bad. One of the roughest Josh Sims, went in my private parlour, sat down with his pint of beer in hand, with six or eight gentlemen, and said he would not leave for anyone, I set the door open, took him by the neck and breeches, and threw him into the passage, he grumbled, but I told him next time he would go out of doors. He was a tall big fellow, but he knew me when I was at Grimsthorpe.

On one occasion we had one hundred and eighty members of a club to dine. What food was left I told the members I would give them for lunch next day. The lunch was set, the navvies rushed in, and before the waiters could enter they had pocketed whole pies, meat, cheese, and in fact everything they could lay their hands on ; and something like the man at the George at Huntingdon, the day Mr. George had his men there to pummel the blues. I saw a man put a knife, fork and spoon up his coat sleeve, I told the waiter, who took it from him and soon bundled the fellow down stairs, such was the case at my house.

At the feast we had races. I had a grey Irish horse, which I entered, rode myself, and won easily.

The following April I took a farm under the Earl of Harborough. The ploughed land was very foul ; I got it clean, and afterwards kept it so, without a fallow. I did not take it until after Lady-day. I could not get away from Bytham until the second week in May. As I took all the fixtures and stock-in-trade at my going in, it was agreed that Mr. Wood, the auctioneer, of Grantham, should draw up an agreement to the effect, that at my leaving everything should be re-taken. But when Mr. White had taken the house and land, he gave me notice that he should not take anything, as Mrs. Ponton the landlady had told him that there was no agreement. I told him I should not allow him to come in on those terms, as I had an agreement and meant to act upon it. The agreement, although not signed, I made answer my purpose. When they found I had an agreement, they forgot whether they had signed it or not. So when the two valuers met Mrs. Ponton's man, Mr. Lawrence of Bourne told my men that Mrs. Ponton the landlady had told him there was no agreement, and he should not go into business ; I had told my men all the particulars, so that we were quite up to Mr. Lawrence. I fetched the agreement and gave it into my man's hands to read ; taking care to keep the two men apart, as Lawrence I found wished to see it, So I placed one on the one side, the

other on the other side, and told my man to read, the other to
stand back. Finding he wanted to get behind, and knowing his
reason, I got between and kept them apart. After it was read
he never thought to ask if it was signed, finding it was drawn up
to the effect. They set to work, and finding I would not go out
until the money was paid, they paid me. I brought out all
my things, gave up the key, and walked off.

After I left the inn I went to Saxby, where I found plenty to
do. Nearly all of the Spring fairs were over, and I wanted
sixty beast as well as sheep, having one hundred and fifty acres
of grass land. My home-close was forty acres. Within the
month I had bought fifty steers and nine cows. All went on
well as I had not a failing beast through the summer. Not so
with the crop. I found the wheat full of bunts ; the other ploughed
land was full of docks. I never saw any so bad, and it gave me
plenty of work through the summer.

In September it began to rain; and for two years we had our
sheep dying with the rot, which was general through the country.
The old hay valued to me was worth little, as Mr. Garner the
steward told me that the tenant went to the Exhibition in 1851,
instead of being at home to see to his hay.

The Earl of Harborough was very kind. He gave me a great
deal of grass out of the park at Stapleford, and always close to the
hall. When he sent for me, he would walk with me and tell me
I could take as much as six or seven good loads of hay.
Knowing he was very particular, I always went with my men
and never left them during the day. He said, " Mr. Dale, you
keep your people so quiet; I have a pleasure in giving you
grass." He also was very kind in giving me venison and game.
He would not allow any tenant to shoot rabbits. I did a
great deal of turf draining when I first went, some of the grass
land being very wet. As he would not give tiles to any one, the

L

rabbits did a deal of damage to the drains.   Although he told his keepers to shoot them when I complained, instead of which, they would be drinking, smoking, and shuffling away their time, rather than do what they ought to do.   But I had a plan by which I could take them out of the drains without ferret or dog.   By beginning to tap at one end of the drain with a spade, the rabbits would all creep to the end which was blocked up.   I very much astonished my daughter Gertrude, when she was at home for her holidays, by taking twenty-six one day in a short time, with nothing more than a spade to tap along the top of the drain ; she was much pleased to help me home with them.   Of course I did not let my men or neighbours know, and Lord Harborough did not object to me doing so.

We went on well until the lung complaint came among our beast, by which I lost thirteen in six weeks.   One I cured ; and another I had killed, and sold it, which got me into a bit of a scrape ; although I did not consider myself that I had done wrong.   I first saw the beast was unwell on Sunday morning; and as I was generally amongst them twice a day, I had him brought home.   I sent for the best man I knew of, who, on examining it, advised me to have it killed, saying it was good meat.   We gave it no medicine, but killed him on the Monday, and sent him to Melton Mowbray on Tuesday. The Inspectors saw it ; and as they knew I had lost several beast, they condemned it, of course, the one being clerk for the Magistrate's Clerk, the other a man who knew but little of meat until it was in his mouth.   I was summoned to appear before the Magistrates next week " for offering meat for sale unfit for the food of man."   I went, taking my witnesses, and found there were three Magistrates.   The Chairman asked me all the questions he thought proper, (he is dead now, so I will not trouble my readers with his name), and then said, " It is a bad case." The Clerk's man (the Inspector) said, " It is, sir." I said " You will hear my witnesses." Mr. Putching of Edenhamthorpe, living near to me, a man of business, occupying a large portion of his own land, and keeping a bailiff; he, being junior Magistrate, said, " What witnesses have you, Mr. Dale?" I said, " I have the veterinary surgeon, who is nearly sixty years old; another who has killed hundreds for Lord Harborough and others; Mr. Pears, a neighbouring farmer and butcher; and Mr. Pacey, a man occupying, I should think, one thousand acres of land, and who, on seeing the carcase hanging up, intended taking some home with him for his own use." He said, " We must have them in." After the veterinary and butcher had given their evidence, Mr. Putching said, " That's enough; you have acted exactly as I should have done; there is no blame attached to you. Gentlemen, we must dismiss the case." I asked for my expenses, and he allowed them; but had it not been for Mr. Putching, I should have been fined and condemned.

I was overseer of the poor for nine years, and parish church-warden for seven; but I had always an enemy in the clerk, as he was a lawyer, and I had employed Mr. Atter of Stamford, in a case of settlement, which offended him, and he did not forget to shew it to me; but that ought not to be. I had a deal of trouble with the auditor, he being a friend of Mr. Lawyer's, but I always beat him by applying to the Poor Law Board. On one occasion, it took six months to settle the case, after which the Board complimented me, and ordered Mr. Auditor to allow the bill.

I had one bullock, which the veterinary gave up as hopeless, so I decided to take it in hand. I took a kettle of boiling

water, poured it on each side and as near the lungs as I could.
I made two large sores or blisters. It cured the beast, and
in time it got fat; although it was bad through the country.
The first case which was notiiced in our parish was a cow. There
were eight cottages, and two cows to each. In November
they were tied up, quite away from any other, and from the
road; fed well, kept well and clean, and attended to by the
women in general. Not a cow had been out or changed. In
March the first fell and died. By July nine of their cows
were dead, although everything possibly was done for them,
but to no purpose. Well, we got over that. The following
harvest my crops were good, having been got in in first-rate
condition. We worked hard, as the weather was all that
could be desired. When in I gave all that helped me, a supper;
and after they had enjoyed themselves, left my house at half-
past twelve. It was a beautiful moonlight night, and some
of the men had to pass the stack-yard. I went to bed very
tired. By half-past one, the stackyard was all in a blaze—
every stack on fire. It must have been the crackling of peas
and corn that woke me, as I was the first to see it, my bedroom window being opposite. .I shall never forget the sight.
I was out as quickly as possible; and after calling all the
children, sent the man to Melton for the engine, but to no
purpose. Being very dry, all was burnt by six o'clock the
next morning. I had not so much straw as would fill my hat.
The Rev. R. Mapleton and his lady were the first to comfort
my family, as they lived close by, and were always very kind.
Mrs. Mapleton stood up to her ancles in water filling the
pails for the men; he doing all that man could do, and for
days did not leave except to go to meals, and then he would
frequently insist that I should go with him. His constant

kindness I shall never forget; and also that of the Earl of Harborough, will never be erased from my memory. He heard all about it in the morning, as his head keeper saw it from his window, and was soon on the spot. About twelve o'clock the Earl sent to say that he wished to see me as soon as I could leave. I rode down at once, the Rev. R. Mapelton saying he would see to everything until I returned, as he wished to know what Lord Harborough thought about it.

As I approached the Hall, the Earl and Countess met me very kindly. He said, "Mr. Dale, I am sorry to hear of your loss." I said, "I will answer any questions you wish." He said "I have not sent for you to question you; I wish to comfort you. Your rent day is next week?" "I said, it is, my lord." He said, " Don't you trouble about that; and I will find you all the keep you want for your stock through the winter, both hay and turnips: send your carts when you want; if you do not, I shall be displeased. Your half-year's rent (£130) I shall not take, and will tell Mr. Hasell all about it." After we had finished our conversation, He said, " Now, go home, and comfort your poor family." I had told him what a kind friend Mr. Mapelton had been. I had not been home more than half-an-hour before his groom rode into the vicarage yard with game and venison. His lordship had not spoken to Mr. M. before.

I now had to take a turn with the principal policeman, from whom I had heard unpleasant words. So I called him in, and shown him in the presence of Mr. Mapleton that I had reduced my insurance to the amount of £100 only the Christmas before, and then ordered him out, telling him to be more cautious of what he said and how he acted, for the future.

The next blow I had was the illness of my fourth daughter. In March, I had her from Stamford, where she was in business, and took her to Doctor Whitchurch of Melton Mowbray. He said Saxby air would do more than his medicine, and as my house stood high, it was very healthy. After a time I took her again, when he said, it was a cold and a little weakness in one lung. She got no better, but lingered on, gradually sinking, and died, October the 10th, 1861. During her illness the Countess was extremely kind in sending game, venison, and fruit; in fact anything she thought she would fancy. Our neighbours were all very kind.

I forgot to say before this that the Earl of Harborough died. Mr. Taylor and myself were the only tenants invited to follow. About two years before, Mr. Garner the steward died. After his death, the Earl appointed R. Hassel, Esq., who was steward for the Earl of Chesterfield, and occuping over a thousand acres of arable land himself and kept a bailiff. One day when he went home, his bailiff told him that they had lost a dung-cart, and thought it would be best to advertise it. He said, " Oh no; we shall run against it some day; keep your eyes open, and you will see it." At the end of the year they were taking the dung out of the yard, and found the cart under it. In his report, after looking over the Earl's estate, he stated that he found the grass land on my farm much improved; and as for the arable, it was greatly enhanced in value. It was in a bad state when I entered; but I had no fallow after the first year.

About two years before I gave up, the Countess thought it better to have a resident steward, who began by making changes. They had eighty acres of very bad land, that had changed hands six times during the ten years I was there. It lay two miles from me; undrained, and three very steep hills to get at it; it was bound together with twitch, and as they would not give a tile, they could not get a tenant for it. He came to me several times and said I must have it. I told him I would not. At last he got quite ill-tempered about it. I told him I would rather give up what I had than take it. He said he had had several applications from farmers, and some if they had mine would take to the pasture, which was the poor land. I refused; but as he had been many times, and finding he meant mischief, I said, " If you will send me a man that will give me one hundred pounds to let him in at Lady-day, I will go out, by your man taking everything at valuation." He said it was unreasonable of me to think of such a thing. And as the Countess did not wish me to leave unless I liked, I told him I should not move without; if he did I would sell my stock off in February."

I thought of putting my youngest daughter, who was then keeping my house, to a business; as I had done with all her brothers and sisters, and I would be quiet for a while.

The Steward one day sent a Mr. Markham to see me about the farm, who knew more about drapery than farming, but having married a woman with some money, came and told his business, but he thought the money too much. I said, " I will not take one shilling less." He said, " What lawyer shall we go to?" I said, " None; you come here on Friday night, and I will write out an agreement, if you do not like it, don't sign it." On Friday night he came, looked it over, and signed it. I sent it on Saturday to Leicester and got it stamped, otherwise I knew he would get laughed at when it was known that he had taken the pasture land; so he was. But between that and Lady-day, he had brought many valuable implements on the premises. At Lady-day he objected to pay the one hundred pounds. We had every thing valued His man held off, and would not settle the business with mine; but they said they would send the account to me in London. The Steward came for the rent before it was due; I finding they were working together, told Markham I should not move until I received the one hundred pounds for the good-will. I told the steward 1 should pay no rent until I had received my tenant-right. As I was under no discharge, and had named all these things in the agreement, Markham said he would fetch all his things away. I dared him to touch a thing until I received the money, and told him I should not move. At the last day he paid it and I let him in. They kept me a long time out of the tenant-right; I told Mr. Ogden my banker, in the presence of the steward, to pay the rent as soon as he received it and not before. At the same time Mr. Ogden satisfied the steward, and told him he need not be afraid.

My Favourite Girls.

Up in the early morn,
   Just at the peep of day,
Straining the milk in the dairy,
   Turning the cows to graze.
Sweeping the floor in the kitchen,
   Making the beds up stairs,
Washing the breakfast service,
   And rubbing the parlour chairs.

Brushing the crumbs from the floor cloth,
　Hunting for eggs in the yard,
Basting the meat for dinner,
　Spinning the linen yarn,
Spreading the unbleached linen
　Upon the new mown sward,
Looking over every meadow,
　Where the wild strawberry grows.

Starching their cottons for Sunday,
　Churning their beautiful cream,
Scouring the pails and the skimmer,
　Near to the running stream,
Feeding the geese and the chickens,
　Making puddings and pies,
Rocking the babies cradle,
　Fanning away the flies.

Grace in every movement,
　Music in every tone,
Beauty in form and feature,
　Hundreds might covet to own,
Cheeks that rival the roses,
　Teeth like the whitest of pearls,
One of my favourite lasses,
　Is worth a score of your dressy girls.

M

CHAPTER VIII.

After spending three weeks with the neighbouring farmers, as I had many kind friends, I left for London. As my friends did not wish me to be idle, I sold beast in Copenhaven Market, until I was laid up and suffered for months with rheumatics; my Doctor said I must give that up, but I was very fond of it. I have rode many miles to look over a good farm, or to see a fine herd of deer.

During my two years as cattle salesman, I found out what before had been a mystery to me. We know that no grazier likes to hear that his beast or sheep were turned out, not sold from the first market they were sent to; although I know such is frequently the case, not because the price of meat is lower, but because the salesman has so much grass keeping near, and sometimes a long way from the market, and if he were not to send stock to eat it, he would not get a profit from the land he had taken. I became well acquainted with both the letter and taker of keep for miles round London. After the hay is got, the eddish is let until after Christmas. I knew some of the large salesmen who take hundreds of acres, and of course the eddish must be eaten or he is the loser; but they ought not to take so much. And as the new sheds are so comfortable and close to the market, beast never ought to be turned out after September. I have known a salesman turn away a good customer for ten shillings in six beast, worth thirty pounds each; those beast were turned out at the end of October, drove three miles to the field, where they were to lay till the next market day. The beast being tired by standing and their feet tender, as soon as they got into the field they laid themselves down on the wet ground. Next morning there they lay at seven o'clock, covered with white rime; two fell lame and could not be got to the market; and when they did go, they were sold for three pounds less money than was bid for them the first day; the others made one pound less per head, and all for the ten shillings bait, or rather, because the salesman had taken so much keep and wanted to make a good profit out of it; he was sure to get all other expenses paid at the grazier's loss. I could name scores of cases of the kind. I know that it is a loss of ten shillings to a grazier to have a bullock turned out from Monday to Thursday, besides other expenses; I think the evil would be remedied, were all to pull together.

A similar bit of business is now carried on at home. If a man has a pig to sell, and lives ten miles from market, it must be put into a cart and sent to market to be honoured with the sight of the auctioneer's hammer; and the expenses all add to the price of meat. The consumer pays for it without benefiting the feeder. I will put the expenses at six shillings, driver of horse and cart one shilling, sixpence toll bar, (if not more,) horse feed and ostler one shilling, feed for boy sixpence; in all nine shillings. Such and similar cases I have frequently witnessed. It is useless for the butcher to go to the feeder as they used to do to buy his meat.

In some parts of our country where the auctioneers have

such holds on the feeders, or rather, where the feeders are deficient in judgment, surely our forefathers would have laughed at the idea. Were the consumers in my way of thinking, they would leave off eating meat, and subscribe to keep our butchers from starving, until the graziers would consent to sell their stock themselves at home, or at market, as before; as it would be a saving in expense, and thus lower the price to the consumer. Let Mr. Auctioneer look out elsewhere as they will take care to be paid well.

I hope I have said enough to set others thinking. I think that by acting together the evil would be remedied. The late I. George, Esq., of Bythorn, grandfather of the present Mr. George, told me that the turn-out system was practised so strongly upon him at one time, that for self defence, he went to the Old Smithfield Market and sold his beast himself. The salesmen did not like it; but as with the election party at Huntingdon, he was not to be beaten. As he fed a large number of beast, he found it a great saving, and his mind was more at rest in the business.

After I recovered from the rheumatics, I met, and made an offer of marriage to my present wife; but no seven years courting this time; we made quick work, as courted and got married in four months. A Cousin of mine having charge of a man-of-war lying off Sheerness, came up to London and invited us down to spend our honeymoon, which we did, and enjoyed it very much. If my lady had have taken it in her head to have run away, she could not go without me; after visiting her friends, who received me very kindly.

When I was young we had a great many Irishmen come over for the harvest work. Hundreds of them were employed in the fens in Lincolnshire. Should the harvest time be wet, the men earned but little. I knew a noble Lord, whom the Irishmen were sure to call upon if they were short of money or unwell; single men that did not care to return so quick, there was always work for them, as he kept a large heap of stones in the yard in front of his house; these men were set to carry them from one side of the yard to the other, and *visa versa*, one by one, on no account to take two at once. There was a man to look after them and report anything he saw amiss; each man at night received his pay according to his time.

The same Nobleman had a very large man for his waggoner, as he kept a noble team of horses; this man used to boast of his strength with a little science, few men dare to encounter him. At the country feast he was the champion. Lord H. as a joke agreed with a prize fighter, the best man he knew at that time in London, to come down to his place as a beggar on tramp in the dusk of the evening; which he did according to agreement, no one being in the secret but themselves. He came and rung the bell, and it was answered by the footman. He asked to speak with his Lordship; the footman denied him, but to no purpose, as he squeezed himself into his Lordship's room, the footman not being able to keep him back. When he got into the room Lord H. appeared surprised, and told the footman to send for the waggoner; who on coming his Lordship told him to put the man out, as he could not suffer him to be there. As the prize man had taken a chair, when the waggoner went towards him he sprung at him and knocked him down, and then sat down again. Lord H. called him a muff, and told him to take hold of him and put him out at once. The waggoner pulled off all his upper clothing and went at the man with all force, but only to be knocked down again. The third time he was served the same; then he said that he must be the very devil, and he would fetch the constable. The footman went in to help him but was served the same. Lord H. then ordered the man food and drink, gave him something and paid him well for his trouble. The man went back by coach to London. His Lordship was much pleased, and did not forget to tell his friends of the joke.

The same Lord H. lost one of his tenants by death, leaving a wife and large family. A neighbour proffered his services for a time to manage for her; then he told the steward she could not keep the farm on as she had but little money, and wished him to tell his Lordship that he would take the farm. The steward told his Lordship, who sent for the farmer, and talked as if he was sure the poor woman could not carry on, and said he did not want the farm untenanted. The farmer said he should like the farm, if his Lordship would cause the widow to be discharged, he would take it. "Ah!" he said to the farmer, "I see you are quite sure the farm wont keep her and the family;" then Lord H. said, "She shall have yours, I will find her money, and a bailiff to manage for her; and instead of her having her discharge, you shall have yours." My readers may judge what a surprise it was to the farmer, after begging and praying found it was no use, it was done. His Lordship saw the motives of the unjust neighbour, and caused the discharge to be carried out for the comfort of the widow and her children. The farmer was so scouted that he left the neighbourhood.

I had a proud, disagreeable neighbour at Saxby. Before I had been there many days, as my man and I were mending the back fence, he rode into my home close, which was forty acres, close by us, without speaking. He had a basket with him, to take mushrooms. After dinner I took a spike, and did the gate up. In the evening I was asked by another to go to his house and smoke a pipe with him; Mr. K. was there also. He said, " Mr. Dale, I see you have spiked the small gate up, next to my field." I said, " I have, sir." He said, "Ah! if Lord Harborough comes, he will soon make you undo it." I said, " Lord Harborough wishes me to keep off all trespassers, and I shall obey his orders."

It passed on like this, he trying all he possibly could to annoy me, for four years. I was frequently asked by the steward to smoke a pipe, and spend the evening with him. All these things were talked over, and then he told his lord-ship, which pleased him much. I always came off victorious, Lord Harborough said he was glad Mr. K. had got his match.

However, an event at length transpired, which succeeded in making us good friends. It was as follows. One evening I was driving along the road, and hearing a loud groan, I stepped out of my conveyance, looked in his field, and saw a fine grey mare, which he had just refused £50 for, on her back in a narrow deep ditch. There had been a good deal of rain; and as the water came down it was stopped by her body, so that in a short time it would soon reach her mouth. I was about a quarter of a mile from home, and his house about two hundred yards from mine. When I got to my house I found my two men waiting for me. I told them to put the horse in the stable, and get the pick-axe, spade, rope, gears, and collar ready, as one of my neighbour's cart horses was in a ditch close by.

I went to his house, and met the boy whom he had just paid, coming from his yard, it being Saturday night. I said, " Tom, is your master at home?" He said, "Yes, sir." I said, "Tell him I want him at once." I knew his temper would not allow him to come out for my order, I waited for a minute and then went to his room, where he was sitting with his legs crossed and smoking his pipe. I said, "If you do not move quickly your grey mare will be drowned." I told him all about it, which caused him to look very white and wild. He said his men were gone two miles away for goods, as we had no shops in the village. I told him that my labourers were ready for the occasion. We passed my house and he could hear the mare groan very loud. We got there just in time, as the top of her head was at the bottom of the ditch, the water had risen near to her mouth which was wide open. Her body was a dam and stopped the water. The first thing I did was to put a halter on her head, so that the men could hold it up, until we dug away the side of the bank; which we did and soon had her out dirty, wet and cold. He asked me what was the best thing to do for her? I said, " Take her home, have her scraped well, rubbed dry, and give her a little gruel in about a hour, with a small portion of food." In the morning the mare was all right. After that he never attempted to treat me unkindly, he was also kinder to others. As a man he was clever and a good scholar, but it was his bad temper that caused the mischief. My readers may be sure we were friends after that. The time my daughter was ill he was very kind to her, and we parted good friends. He always made any of my family welcome and was pleased with their company at his house; he has frequently invited me to go and see him. The poor man is now dead, which is the reason I do not give his name in full. I hope he is happy, as we all hope and must try to be.

CHAPTER IX.

Upon my return to Kimbolton, in the year 1864, I found eight or nine of the old labourers and some of my friends, who having heard that I was coming back, were there ready to receive me and help me in with my goods. I had been away many years, and I saw a great change in them all, as I have no doubt they did in me, for old age will creep on. I found many of my old friends very kind. There was only one of the old school left. When I came here ~~forty three~~ *seven* years back, we used to receive many kind invitations from Mr. and Mrs. Ainsworth at the rectory.

The first time I took my wife to see the hounds meet in front of the castle she was quite delighted with the sight. After they were started and out of view, I walked towards the park and the house in which I had lived twenty-two years. On our way I showed her the mark in the tree made by the bullet which was so near killing the good old Duke, when up came the present Duke with the Hon. George Fitzwilliam. The Duke took his cigar from his mouth, spoke very kindly, and asked me how long I was going to stay at Kimbolton. I told him that I hoped to spend the rest of my days here. I introduced

N

my present wife, and told him I was going to show her the
lodge and farm if we might be allowed.   He very kindly said,
" You can find your way well about ; go where you like."
I thanked him and parted.

One day when we were walking near Stow, and it being
near sun set, we walked along towards a pond bank, so as we
could see it go down in the West.   It was in September ; and
all at once I saw a fine leveret sitting close to us in the grass.
I at once put my foot on it, and you can judge the surprise
of my wife when she heard it.   I need not tell my readers
what became of the poor thing.   I have done the same thing
when the dogs have been hunting, and when we have been
shooting.

I had not been long at Kimbolton, before I paid a visit to
the Rev. Thomas Ainsworth.   About three o'clock in the
afternoon he said he was quite beaten out, and thought he
should have to leave.   He could not get any one to take
his curate in, and what to do he did not know, as he had been
all over the parish, so he asked me if I could assist him.   I
told him that I would ask my wife.   We agreed to take the
one coming—Rev. P. P. Mason, who was with us over
two years.   We liked him, and got on well ; and sometimes a
joke passed between us which made it very nice.   We had
two keys to the door, so that when he went out to dine,
which he frequently did, he could let himself in.

One day my wife and I, with Mr. and Mrs. Margerrison,
went to pay a visit to our good old friend Mr. Mash of
Stow, where we met with a jolly party, and did not get home
until one o'clock the next morning.   I being jolly, as I always
am when I go there a shooting, sang my favourite song, which
runs as follows :—

WHEN WE WENT OUT A SHOOTING.

Some friends of mine for mirth and glee,
Fixed on a day to have a spree,
When it was agreed upon that we
   Should all go out a shooting:
There were Will Smith and Stephen Shore,
With Harry Grant and Bobby Blore,
Besides old Muggins and Dicky Moore,
I think in all full half-a-score:
It was in the autumn's dreary close,
When frost begins to nip the toes,
These friends of mine they did propose
   We should go out a shooting.
Chorus—With powder, wadding, dog, and gun,
      Up, sportsman, up, the day's begun,
      I never shall forget the fun
      We had going out a shooting.

It was at old Muggins' house we met,
All ripe for fun, a jovial set,
To have a cigar and just a wet
   Before we went out shooting:
Old Muggins, he a musket had,
Which was his father's when a lad,
Whilst Bob Blore made a pretty fuss
About his uncle's blunderbuss:
Determined all things should be right,
We primmed and loaded over night,
And full four hours before 'twas light
   We started out a shooting.
Chorus—With powder, &c.

N2

As we were going down Fenchurch Street
Towards Saint George's church to get,
A lot of the new police we met
    As we were going a shooting :
The sergeant quick did collar me,
The others, the guns when they did see,
Cried out, " Lads ; he's a burglar, he,
What's in those bundles come let's see !
With that a dreadful fight arose,
Poor Muggins got a broken nose,
Then off to the Station-house we goes
    Instead of going a shooting.
Chorus—With powder, &c.

We then by paying something each,
As we for freedom did beseech,
We did contrive to heal the breach,
    And started off a shooting :
Every thing then went on well,
No pleasure sure could ours excel,
Until we came near Camberwell,
Where we a precious fog did smell :
So thick, and in such clouds arose,
Like cobwebs they hung on our clothes,
Not one saw a yard before his nose
    As we were going a shooting.
Chorus—With powder, &c.

But it seems misfortunes follow nigh,
For as we crossed o'er Peckham Rye,
Bob poked his gun in Bill Smith's eye
    As we were going a shooting :

So dark and dismal was the fog,
Poor Muggins fell into a bog,
His gun went off and shot his dog
As dead as any wooden log:
When he again on dry ground stood,
We laughed, tho' forced to chew the cud,
To see his mouth stuffed full of mud
   Through going out a shooting,
Chorus—With powder, &c.

We halted just about day break,
As all our legs began to ache.
Thinking some refreshments we would take
   E'er we commenced our shooting:
Upon a stile when safely moored,
Of beef we had a perfect hoard,
The gin and water we had stored.
Into our tumblers then we poured;
But it seems misfortune never halts,
For Muggins' wife, who had her faults,
Instead of gin had put up salts
   For us to take out shooting.
Chorus—With powder, &c.

As misfortune still did follow on,
Game we could not happen upon,
We all agreed to go back home,
   And bid farewell to shooting:
For my part I can only say,
I never spent so sad a day,
For birds—black, white, or grey,
I never saw one all the way:

Now, Muggins sits at home and crams,
Sells his butter, eggs, and hams,
But sporting always he condemns
    Since the day we went out shooting.
Chorus—With powder, &c.

After having spent a pleasant evening we returned home,
and on arriving opposite our door, Mr. Margerrison pulled
up, and as I was sitting behind with my wife, I sprung from
the trap, and said, "Now my dear, come on;" thinking to
take her; but she being too heavy, or I too weak, I fell
backwards and she upon me. There we lay; Mr. and Mrs.
Margerrison laughing at us. The Rev. Mason came to the
window; he also laughed, and said, I should not go to
Stow any more. As it took me a little time to unlock the
door, he joked me about it afterwards. I thought I would
play him a joke; so one night when he had gone out to
dine, I went to bed, (but not to sleep,) and left the key in
the lock, which was a spring one. About eleven o'clock he
came home, and I heard him trying to unlock the door; but
of course he could not as the key was in the lock. The
policeman, who happened to be passing at the time, tried,
but with no better success. Next, came the porter from the
Duke's gates with his lantern, and he tried to get the key in,
but in vain. I opened the window, and said, " What is
the matter." He said, " You must come down and open the
door, as we cannot unlock it." I went down, took my key
out quietly and quickly with my left hand, put it in my
pocket, opened the door a little way, and said, " Give me the
key and let me have a try." They said, " It is of no use."
The Rev. Gentleman wanted to pass, but I would not allow

him until he gave me the key. I put it in the lock in an instant, worked it backwards and forwards, and said, " Why, you have been to Stow." I then let him, in and he went to bed. It has been a mystery to them all ever since, which this little book will explain, as I intend to send him one when it is complete. He has now got a living, and is very comfortable; but unfortunately he has lost his wife, who, as I was told, was a very nice lady.

Since I have been here, I have had two daughters married by the Rev. Hope Grant. At the marriage of the last, the Rev. Hope Grant, the Right Hon. Lord Mandeville, and Captain Welstead honoured us with their company at the wedding breakfast. Since then, I have buried my third daughter, Emma; she had been poorly for some time, and in March, 1870, she was a little better; but the Prince and Princess of Wales being on a visit to the Duke and Duchess of Manchester, and as the Oakley hounds were to meet in front of the castle, she and thousands of others went to see them and a large number of ladies and gentlemen of the day, where she caught a fresh cold, from which she never recovered, but died on the twelfth of September, in the same year. I am thankful she died happy. She was kindly attended by the Rev. Hope Grant and Doctor Hemming, whom I am sure did their best to heal and comfort her in both body and soul.

I had not had a day's hunting for some time, and as the Prince and Princess with the Duke and Duchess and a large company were to meet the Fitzwilliam's hounds at Great Catworth road, I and a friend of mine had two horses lent to us for the occasion. My friend's name was Mr. James Lintott, son of J. Lintott, Esq., of the firm of Foster and Smith, and is now a pupil of Mr. Wallis, farm bailiff to His Grace the Duke of Manchester.

Afterwards, the hounds and the thousands of people that were present left the place of meeting for Hunts Closes, where they soon found a fox and started off at a slashing rate.   Mr. Lintott not being very well at the time, and as his horse was a hard-mouthed brute it became unmanageable, and soon proved too much for its rider, and I might not have seen more of him, had not the hounds ran in a half circle and came to a check, when I heard a gentleman say, " There's a man down," and on looking round, I saw my friend Mr. Lintott on the ground, and a doctor and six other gentlemen rendering him their assistance   As I was approaching them I heard one say, " Do you know who he is ?"   They replied, " No."   As soon as I reached them I dismounted and said, " I am much obliged to you gentlemen ; he is a friend of mine, and by your leaf I will take charge of him." He was quite unconscious at the time, but whether it was a fit or the result of the fall no one knows.   I am inclined to think that as the horse was very hard mouthed it got the better of its rider, who not being very well at the time, swooned and fell ; but I believe it did him good as he has not been unwell since.

A gentleman caught his horse and brought it to us, when we mounted him and proceeded on our way to a new farm house, which was just before we reached Covington.   I left him there and took his horse with mine, and as soon as I arrived home, sent a conveyance back for him.   Meantime, the lady bathed his head and face, and afterwards gave him some tea and anything that he wished for.   Mr. Lintott arrived home about two hours after I did, when Doctor Hemming was ready to attend him, and by his kind treatment was well in a few days.   Both ladies and gentlemen from the castle were very kind in coming to enquire after him.   I heard that there were nine others who met with a fall the same day ; and not to be wondered at either, considering the large quantity of people that were out on the occasion. The Prince rode well, and the Princess looked noble and happy in her carriage.

Since then I have taken my wife and Mr. Lintott down to look over the Grimsthorpe estate, which is very large, with fine park, and noble castle. It has changed hands four times since I left forty-three years ago. The name of Willoughby de Ersby is now extinct. The castle and estate is now in the hands of the Dowager Lady Aveland. The fish ponds are very large; the park and grounds are very extensive; and the wood, plantations, and gardens are of great size. My wife and friend very much enjoyed it. As I had not been there for several years, we paid a visit to some of my old friends, viz: Mr. Pilkerton, by whom, with his usual kind hospitality, we were well entertained; and Mr. and Mrs. Clark, as they were of the old school, and good farmers. I saw two fine blood-red cows of Mr. Pilkerton's—mother and her daughter with her first calf—from which they gathered twenty-six pounds of butter the week we were there. He told me he had been bid thirty pounds for the cow. We were also kindly received by Mr. and Mrs. Caswell of the Willoughby Arms Hotel, Little Bytham. Their kind attention to their customers seemed to be gaining and bringing them much custom, and they are highly respected, which is a proof of their moderate charge, which I also witnessed at the time we were there. I had not seen Mr. Caswell for some years, and I was quite surprised to see him so much after the style of Daniel Lambert. In the morning we went to Little Bytham church, looked round the church-yard, and read the names and verses on the gravestones of my father, mother, eldest and youngest brother. I had the honor of walking with the oldest gentleman but one in the village,

O

whose name was Mr. Nixon, and a fine gentleman he was in his young day.   He was in the Cavalry, and looked very noble in his regimentals.   We called to see Mrs. Parnard and her daughter, whom we found looking well; but like my wife and I, they began to show old age.   I also showed them the old stone wall, in which I kept my money when a lad; and where old Mrs. Split-plum lived.

In the afternoon, we went with Mrs. and Miss Caswell to Careby, to hear the Rev. I. Reynardson preach in his parish church.   I was quite astonished to see the alterations that had taken place, and the improvements which they had made on the Rev. Gentleman's house, pleasure grounds, green houses, vinery, and his aviary, with beautiful piece of water, is beyond praise.

The water in front of his house was stocked with all kinds of foreign ducks, both small and great, of various colours.   I have been to many noblemen's seats, but I never saw anything like those ducks.

The foreign pheasants in the aviary were very handsome; they were also very quiet and tame, and seemed to enjoy themselves.   A few years back the ground was all waste on which these places now stand, and near to the church it was quite unsightly.   As my grandmother lived in the village I remember the place quite well, and was quite delighted to see the improvement made by the great alterations that had taken place.

We also had the pleasure of looking at two lots of short-horned beast that were grazing on some good land on both sides of the vicarage, belonging to I Berridge, Esq.: altogether, the sight was grand; and I never expected to see the like at Careby, which we did by the kind permission of the worthy rector.

During my stay at Little Bytham, I drove my wife and Mr. Lintott through Witham-on-the-Hill, and showed them the old school, blacksmith's shop, the post at the end of the village, where I was chased to by Mr. Gattlief the schoolmaster, where he gave up the chase. This occurred at the finish of my education.

When we left Little Bytham we travelled by rail to Peterborough, where we spent one night with our worthy friend, Mr. J. Shrives and his good lady, in Broad Bridge Street, who, three years ago, left my youngest son in New Zealand, and very sorry they were to part with him, as they wrote and told me afterwards. We looked round the Cathedral and town, and after having been kindly treated by Mr. and Mrs. Shrives, we left for Huntingdon by the Great Northern, and from there to Kimbolton by the Midland; and on arriving there, a grand mistake occurred—there being no regular conveyance to meet the afternoon train, but there was a fly standing there with the door open and the driver against the horse, which I was pleased to see, and went up to him and asked if he had got room; and on him replying that he had, my wife and I jumped in, and Mr. Lintott got up and rode by the side of the driver, who shut to the door and drove us down to Kimbolton. When we arrived at J. Beedham's, Esq., the solicitor, the gates were open, and to our surprise, we were drove in. I heard Mr. Lintott tell the driver that we did not live there. He said, " All right; I know that." I thinking he might have a parcel or something to leave there, so sat quiet. The servants were summonsed by the ring of the door-bell; and the driver jumped down and opened the poor; when I said, " What does all this mean? He said, " You are Lawyer Beedham, are you not? I said, " Certainly, not; you have drove by

o2

my house, which is in High Street; you have seen me many times; and I believe you saw me talking with your master, Mr. Craddock, the day before we left Kimbolton, and I should have thought you would have known me again." He said, "Well, I ought to have brought Mr. Beedham." I said, "Well, you may drive us home now," which he did. Mr. Craddock and I having to settle the affair afterwards. The only thing that troubled me was, to think that Mr. Beedham would have to walk home, a distance of two miles and-a half, and it being a hot day would help to make it worse. It appears that he came by a train that was going to Huntingdon, and arrived at Kimbolton about five minutes after we had left. The fly had been ordered and sent expressly for him. Mr. Beedham very kindly excused me of any blame, and laughed at the joke; but not so with Mr. Craddock, though we are now friends.

After I had been at Kimbolton some time, I proposed to the Duke that the Ornamental Waters in front of the castle should be stocked with fish, as I found out by his conversation that he was fond of fresh-water fish. He said he should not mind the expense if I could obtain suitable stores. There were some very good ones when he left for Jamaica, but as he had been away twenty-one years they had all disappeared. He thought they might have been netted or taken in some way or other by intruders, and such might have been the case; but if the ice was not broken every morning during the sharp frosts in the winter to admit air, they would all die. He said, "Well, it might be so; and I should like you to take it in hand and see after it." I did so, and he gave me all the assistance I needed, and in a few years we had some splendid fish: such as tench, carp, perch, eels, and in one or two ponds, some fine pike. We have taken some out of the bason that have weighed as much as fourteen pounds. But when I went there, the fish, what few there were, were like the deer—very small; and so was everything else belonging to William, the fifth Duke of Manchester. Afterwards the fish were fed properly. The gardeners frequently took two or three hundred wasps' nests during the summer, which were thrown away, and for which they received sixpence for every nest, which the head gardener entered in his account to the Duke. As soon as the gardener found out that I ordered his men to put the young wasps and worms in the ponds as food for the fish, he being a cross grained fellow, would not allow his men to go after or take them; the consequence was, he lost a great deal of his best fruit. The Duke, on asking me why the wasps were not destroyed as usual, I told him; and also informed him that they were worth all the money as food for the fish, as well as saving his fruit. He then said, " Never mind the gardener; you set men to do it and allow them the usual price, and enter it in your account; it will be all the same to me." I did so; which soon put things to rights on that point, and the Duke was very pleased. When he saw the fish come to fed on the young wasps, he could, with a cast net, take a dish of eels at any time he thought proper.

I did not inform my readers that my first dog, 'Pilot,' was bred and given to me by Squire Handley of Cubberthorpe. He was by a Newfoundland dog out of a Tiger-hound-bitch, and was taken from his mother the day after he was pupped, put into a man's pocket, carried over forty miles on horseback, and was reared by my wife's mother with a quill and new milk out of a bottle, as a lamb. He was brought to me at Kimbolton when he was nine months old, and as he was so lanky and ill-looking, although a black tan and smooth in the hair, I was almost ashamed to show him to the Duke; but at two years old I never saw a finer dog. In the summer time, when he was out of condition for work, he weighed eight stone, (fourteen pounds to the stone,) weighed by Mr. Giddings. He was a splendid retriever, and we seldom lost a head of game, as his nose was so good. The game was never injured by other dogs, as he was master, all others kept a respectable distance from him when he made his appearance. When he was seven years old; as he was running after a rabbit that I had shot, and which had tippled into the middle of a brier bush, he ran his head with such force against a small tree which was growing in the bush, the stem of which was not so thick as my wrist, that he put his neck out of joint and was dead in an instant, and so there was an end of my good dog ' Pilot.' Fortunately, I had one of his breed about nine months old, which I soon began to try, by putting him on the boar that we kept, and he turned out as well as we could expect for his size.

Having heard from Lord Mandeville of Mr. Grantly Berkeley's bet about taking five full headed bucks in one day, with one dog and two horses, and his horse to lie down during the performance. I set to with my horse, and in a few days I had taught him to drop at the word of command, but as it was a useless practice I did not follow it up. I may as well add that the Hon. Grantly Berkeley lost his bet, as the first buck the dog was put on to, turned on him and stabbed him in the shoulder, and he had to be carried out of the park; I believe he sent for other dogs, and completed his task, but he lost his bet.

A short time back, Mrs. Dale and I were invited to dine

with my old friend, Mr. Mash of Stow, he told me his wool buyer was coming to pack and take away all his wool. I, always being fond of the wool trade, and having had great practice when young, I went to help them, and got there about two o'clock, when they had just begun. I told them they would have no time to spare, and as we were going to dine at three, I advised them not to stop to smoke until they had finished. By half-past seven in the evening, they had packed twenty-three sheets, some of which contained over twenty-three tods, and all were nearly up to that weight. The wool was packed, sheets sewn up and weighed, at over two pounds per todd, and the money taken before eight o'clock. The business which passed off capitally, was all done by five of Mr. Mash's sons, and Mr. James Horsford of Dean, who is a fine young man, and a few others who assisted in the work, over which there was plenty of ale and no unpleasant words. After which we had a good spread, with plenty of wine and liquor, which made us all very jolly through the evening, and we wished them good night at eleven o'clock.

Mr. Mash is one of the best and largest farmers and buyers of wool, in this Neighbourhood; and he is very unlike a Leicester buyer, named Pool, to whom I had sold my wool several times while at Saxby, who had a large number of sheets, which he had filled with all sorts of rubbish, straw and chaff; he then went to his banker's and told him that he required a thousand pounds more money. The banker sent a man to look at his stock, who on returning, assured the banker that Mr. Pool had in his warehouse, which was a very large one, a great number of sheets full. After Pool received the money he went away without paying for a great deal he had bought and sent to market. I have not heard of him since.

Mr. Martin of Spaldwick bet Mr. George Cant five pounds that he could not produce a pony from Kimbolton to trot as fast as his. Mr. C. took the bet, and the next morning he looked out for the Rev. J. Hog, dissenting minister. At that time he was about seventy years of age and very eccentric. About ten o'clock when he saw him coming, he hung a fine hare up in the front of his shop, and tied a white cloth round his knee. Mr. Hog said, " Good morning." Mr. Cant said, " Good morning, Sir ;" at the same time hopping towards the Rev. Gentleman, who said, " Oh dear, what lame ?" Mr. C. said, " Yes, Sir, its a bad job." Mr. Hog, said, " What a fine hare you have there." Mr. C. said, " Yes, Sir ; it is very fine, and I would give it to anyone who would lend me a pony to ride to Spaldwick on, as I have very urgent business there this morning." The Rev. Gentlemen said, " What, Mr. Cant ; did you say you would give that hare for the loan of a pony for a few hours ? " Mr. Cant said, " Yes, Sir." Mr. Hog then said, " You may have my ' Billy,' (that was the name of his pony,) but send the hare up first." He sent the hare to his house, and had the pony. Rode over to Spaldwick, won the five pounds, and he was at home again in about three hours ; as ' Billy ' was decidedly the fastest trotter in the County.

After that, Mr. Martin bet Mr. Horsford of Stow, a friend of mine, and large occupier under the Duke, that he dare not appear mounted in scarlet at the meet of the Earl Fitzwilliam's hounds, on the following Wednesday. The bet was a rump of beef and a dozen of wine. At the same time he offered to lend him scarlet ; Mr. Horsford accepted the bet and rode home in the scarlet, leaving his coat at Mr. Martin's. After he had been at home some time, talking over the business of the day with Mrs. H. and Sons, he recollected that he had left in his coat, his pocket book which contained a large sum of money, that he had taken for wheat and other things in the day. His son John was started off to fetch the coat. At first Mr. Martin refused to give it up until his scarlet was returned, but being informed of the money that was in it, he gave it up at once. The following Wednesday morning, Mr. Horsford appeared at the meet in scarlet, and well mounted, as at that time he had a first-rate horse ; the Duke was there, shook hands with him, and was highly amused at the joke.

Once, while I was staying with a friend at Melton Mowbray, we were walking towards the toll-gate in the early hours of the morning, when we met a man with a ladder in one hand, and a pot of red paint and a brush in the other, accompanied by two men with a donkey. The man with the ladder then put it against the upper window of the toll-bar house, when the other two came up with the donkey and called out ' gate !' and as soon as the collector put his head out of the window, his face and white nightcap with tassel, were all plastered over with red paint. I was afterwards told that the collector had offended the then Marquis of Waterford, and that it was he and two noble Lords with the paint and donkey.

The same noble Marquis one night bet that he had a horse in his stable that would walk up stairs and jump over a hurdle in the dining room. The room was cleared, and the hurdle set across the middle of it, the horse was then sent for which walked up stairs, leaped the hurdle, and of course the bet which was very heavy was won. These and many other such like things was the Marquis's delight. He would frequently thrash the policemen, but he was always kind to them afterwards ; in fact he was very liberal with his money to all, which caused him to be much beloved by his fellow men, and as he was immensely rich it seemed a pleasure to him to

P

give some away.

I was once staying at Oakley in the late Duke of Bedford's time, when a nest of partridge's eggs was mown out and brought to Mr. Perkins the keeper, who at once divided them, went down on his hands and knees, and asked me to put a sheep's skin over him, he then crept quietly to two partridges which had been sitting about the same time, and gently put a portion of the eggs under each bird, without disturbing either; this being a much better plan, and less trouble than bringing them up by hand. I have since done the same thing with success.

As soon as the Great Northern Railway was opened, Mr. John Sharp of Little Bytham, was going to London, and he asked Mr. Frank Harris if he would go with him, and he said he would. Mr. Harris, who was upwards of fifty years of age, had never been to London before; he was no scholar but a very good farmer, and a man of large property. When they arrived at Kings' Cross Station, Mr. Sharp slipped away from Mr. Harris, who had lost sight of him, and he began to call for Mr. S., and asked of the persons near, if any of them had seen John Sharp, when all the people looked astonished, but no one answered him. He then said, " Has any of you seen John Sharp ?" They all looked again, but no one answered. He then said, " I say, Policeman, they told me to ask you if I got wrong; have you seen John Sharp ?" The Policeman said, " I don't know who you mean, Sir." He said, " Dang you, I thought everybody new John Sharp : why, John Sharp of Little Bytham, to be sure, he is going to see Lord Willoughby, he is his butcher." Mr. Sharp then came up and apologized for leaving him. They went away in a *crab*, as Mr. Harris told us when he came back, he not remembering the name of a cab. He said the next day they went to Vauxhall in a *blunderbuss*, and quite enjoyed themselves. Of course his tale amused us, and caused a good deal of laughing, in which he joined.

I had a friend at Saxby who was living with an old farmer his uncle, who was very rich. They had a sow which had pigged, and was very ill, and a few days after they thought of giving her a drink, but did not know how. One morning about two o'clock the uncle called out, "Stephen; yah, mun; get up, I've thought of a scheme, call Will, and come here!" Stephen answered, " Yes, uncle." So they went to the old man's room, who said, " Yah, mun; take that drink, go in the stack yard, take a gate head, put it in the sow's mouth, and pour the drink down her throat." They did so at once; and when it was done the sow was dead, as they had choked her. " D.——, boy," Stephen said to the man; " we've done it; don't yah say anything, I can do it." When they went in, the uncle said, " Well, how is she?" Stephen said, " All right, uncle; very quiet." He said, " Ah, I thought that would ease her." They went to bed for about one hour, and then were called again, as they had to feed, clean, and get their horses ready for plough, and be in to breakfast by six o'clock. So when that time arrived, the uncle called from his bedroom and said, " Well, Stephen; how's the sow." " All right, uncle; very quiet." He said, " That's good; I thought it would do." But when he got up at seven, he found out the secret and never forget to tell Stephen of it.

A lady friend of mine, while visiting at Peterborough, received a letter from a friend of hers at Kimbolton, who had been taken ill and wished to see her. On reading the letter, up she got, and could not finish her breakfast as she must go at once. Her daughter said, " Nonsense; there is no train until such a time, and if you do not sit down and finish your breakfast, I will not let the man take you and your luggage to the station." So she sat down, but all on the shake to be off. The time came and off she went. She had such a great deal to tell her fellow passengers about all her troubles and poor Mr. R. who was so anxious to see her, that she passed Huntingdon station where she ought to have stopped, and banged away with her tongue, until she reached Hatfield, when she asked if it was Huntingdon, as she had to get out there. The passengers then told her of her mistake, and advised her to get out there and wait for the next down train; but no, she would not stop there alone, and so she went on to London. She started back again by the next train and fell asleep on the way, passed St. Neots station where she intended stopping, and when she got to Huntingdon she found out her mistake; she then hired a fly and got to Kimbolton at two o'clock the next morning, instead of three the day before.

During the time that I was with the Duke, the brewer called Old Croger, used to go round to all the cellars at the Castle to taste the ale when he liked, always taking a pitcher with him to bring out a little for his lunch. On his return to the butler's pantry, the footman took his quid of tobacco, which he always placed in the lining of his cap, and laid the cap in the window opposite the cellar door; whilst he was in the cellar and having his lunch, the footman opened the quid, filled the inside with cayenne pepper, and put it back in its place; the old man finished his lunch, put the quid in his mouth; but before he had got twenty yards, he met the Duke and me, and with talking and sucking hard his mouth began to get uncomfortable, and he soon began to stamp and swear. The Duke laughed; but Old Croger never left his quid in his cap again.

One evening I was standing at the door of my house at the park farm, when a fine stag passed me, going towards the castle at a fast pace. I ran down at once and told the

Duke, Duchess, and Lady Olivia Montague; we then went in the saloon and saw him pass. The Duchess and I were for shooting, him, and to have him stuffed for the White Hall; but the Duke said, " No, we will get him a companion." I told His Grace I was sure he would not stop. The Duke thought he would; but next morning he was gone; and as Woburn, the seat of the Duke Bedford, was only twenty miles distant, we thought it might have come from there. When I wrote to the park keeper, it appeared they had found him in the woods, and had caught him. We were then glad we did not shoot him.

I have twice in my life caught bucks when they have been asleep, having had the wind in my favour.

I once left my dog Pilot to watch a trap from Saturday night to Sunday night, which Mr. Ibbs and I had found while walking round the farm. The trap had a stoat in it, which I took out and re-set it, the dog looking on all the while. Mr. Ibbs said, " How the dog watches your moves." I said, " He would lie by and watch the trap, if I were to tell him." He said, " Tell him." I told the dog what to do, and there he laid for over twenty-hours, and I had to fetch him home.

When I was about fourteen years of age I was on a visit to my uncle John Dale at Witham-on-the-Hill, it being the village feast, and in the early part of November. About eleven o'clock at night, as it was very dark, my uncle proposed that five others (who were about the same age as I was,) and myself should go into a grass field that was close by and have a game. I then got the flint and steel and started off as fox, but it was so dark that the other boys could not see me ten yards from them. Occasionally I struck a light with the flint and steel, when they would run to the spot, but I was away; and so on for some time; and not a word or sound was heard from either party. After a little time I heard a light cart coming along the road parallel with the field ; I then ran to the hedge opposite the driver, (who was Mr. Charles Brown, and who had left his wife at the feast and was returning home to Lound,) who, as soon as he saw the light, started his horse into a galop ; but I soon headed him, and when opposite the gate I struck a second light, which so frightened Mr. Brown, that he turned his horse sharp round, drove back to his father's where he had left his wife, and told them he had been shot at twice. He stayed at his father's all night, as he dare not attempt to go home again. The next day the parish constable was acquainted with the affair, and a handsome reward was offered for the apprehension of the would-be highwayman. The game was soon known, and Mr. Brown was laughed at and called a coward.

A lady friend of ours advertised for a nurse-maid, when several would-be young ladies applied for the situation ; but each found there would be duties to perform, and also that Mrs. Coots did not intend keeping servants merely for show. Several declined the situation, as they thought three children too many to look after. At last one came, who Mrs. Coots thought looked like business, as she said her papa and mamma could not afford to keep her at home ; but after being told that she would have to take the children out for a walk every day if the weather was fine, she said she could not think of doing that, as she was sure her mamma would wish her to take her daily walks alone ; so under those circumstances she declined the situation ; but I can assure my readers it is a very comfortable one, as Mr. and Mrs. Coots are very nice persons.

At this time I have had the pleasure of having a visit paid me by Mrs. Bishop and Mrs. Wansbro—daughters of my old friend, Mr. J. Dyson, who is after the style of Mr. L. J. Ibbs, who had a pleasure ni giving a first-rate glass of ale to his friends. I and other friends have frequently been invited to Mr. Dyson's and have spent some jolly evenings there. He was highly respected, and served the late Duke of Manchester and his father many years; as did Mr. Ibbs. My order was to see that they and all the tradespeople in Kimbolton had some game during the season, and most of them received a little venison also. The Duke said it caused all of us to unite and be good friends; as union is strength, and so it was, for we could balance any thing at that time.

When the late Duke of Manchester was Lord Mandeville, and was staying on a visit with the late Lady Olivia Sparrow at Brampton park, and during his stay the hounds met at Brampton wood, and as His Grace was fond of hunting, and a bold rider, he went and had a day's run with them; and in the evening Tom Wells, his groom, was summoned to the chapel to prayers, in which he was soon asleep; and at the commencement of one of the hymns, he called out, " Tally-o; there he goes ;" when he was quickly ordered out. The next morning he caught a severe reprimand from His Grace, who told him it would have sounded much better in Brampton wood than in Lady Olivia Sparrow's chapel.

The grandfather of the present Duke of Manchester was pleased to tell his daughters when they were young the following tale :—They used to take a pleasure in asking the clerk of the parish to dine on a Sunday at the castle. One very hot day after he had been dining there, in the middle of the afternoon service he fell asleep and began to snore; the congregation all looking at him, the sexton went and gave him a nudge, whereupon he called out, " I will take another horn, for it is rare beer ;" but to his surprise he received a pat on the top of his head from the parson.

A more awful affair than either of the two preceding ones

was told by the late Col. Steele, as follows :—A footman of his one day took a dish from the room with a bit of beef steak upon it, when, as soon as he had left the room, he put the piece of steak into his mouth; but some person coming upon him quickly, he attempted to swallow it, when it stuck in his throat, and he was dead in a few minutes.

The late Lord Frederick Montague, when about nineteen years of age, asked me to go with him to Milchbourne, as he had received an invitation from the Right Hon. Lord St. John for a day's shooting, to which I consented, and hired a horse and gig of Mr. William Ibbs of the George Hotel for the occasion. On arriving home at night about eleven o'clock, we were told by the second gardener, who kept the gates, that he dare not let us in, as the head gardener had ordered him not to let us in if we were not home by ten. As the Duke was not at home at the time, the head gardener and his wife had charge and lived in the castle. The man at the gates did not open them until Lord Frederick gave orders to the hostler, who happened to come up at the time, to fetch a crow-bar, which he did, and was about to force the gates open. On the Duke's return, which was very soon after, the head gardener and his wife were discharged. Now, after the lock out from the castle, I must bid my readers farewell.

> What man is he who seeketh God,
>   Who seeks and does not find,
> Then let us try to do our best,
>   And not be left behind.

THE AUTHOR.

www.ingramcontent.com/pod-product-compliance
Lightning Source LLC
LaVergne TN
LVHW081346060426
835508LV00017B/1438